NEW DIRECTIONS FOR COMMUNITY COLLEGES

Arthur M. Cohen
EDITOR-IN-CHIEF

Florence B. Brawer
ASSOCIATE EDITOR

Promoting Community Renewal Through Civic Literacy and Service Learning

Michael H. Parsons
Hagerstown Junior College

C. David Lisman
Community College of Aurora

EDITORS

Number 93, Spring 1996

JOSSEY-BASS PUBLISHERS
San Francisco

ERIC®

Clearinghouse for Community Colleges

PROMOTING COMMUNITY RENEWAL THROUGH CIVIC LITERACY AND SERVICE LEARNING
Michael H. Parsons, C. David Lisman (eds.)
New Directions for Community Colleges, no. 93
Volume XXIV, number 1
Arthur M. Cohen, Editor-in-Chief
Florence B. Brawer, Associate Editor

ISSN 0194-3081   ISBN 0-7879-9868-0

NEW DIRECTIONS FOR COMMUNITY COLLEGES is part of The Jossey-Bass Higher and Adult Education Series and is published quarterly by Jossey-Bass Inc., Publishers, 350 Sansome Street, San Francisco, California 94104-1342 in association with the ERIC Clearinghouse for Community Colleges. Second-class postage paid at San Francisco, California, and at additional mailing offices. POSTMASTER: Send address changes to New Directions for Community Colleges, Jossey-Bass Inc., Publishers, 350 Sansome Street, San Francisco, California 94104-1342.

SUBSCRIPTIONS for 1996 cost $49.00 for individuals and $81.00 for institutions, agencies, and libraries.

THE MATERIAL in this publication is based on work sponsored wholly or in part by the Office of Educational Research and Improvement, U.S. Department of Education, under contract number RI-93-00-2003. Its contents do not necessarily reflect the views of the Department, or any other agency of the U.S. Government.

EDITORIAL CORRESPONDENCE should be sent to the Editor-in-Chief, Arthur M. Cohen, at the ERIC Clearinghouse for Community Colleges, University of California, 3051 Moore Hall, 405 Hilgard Avenue, Los Angeles, California 90024-1521.

Cover photograph © Rene Sheret, After Image, Los Angeles, California, 1990.

TCF Manufactured in the United States of America on Lyons Falls Pathfinder Tradebook. This paper is acid-free and 100 percent totally chlorine-free.

CONTENTS

EDITORS' NOTES

The Chinese language has long been celebrated for its symbolic power. For example, the concept *crisis* is composed of two pictographs—danger and hidden opportunities. These ideas aptly describe American society at the end of the twentieth century. Many of our social institutions are under siege, yet we have demonstrated the capability, time and again, to turn crisis into accomplishment.

R. Freeman Butts, former professor at Columbia University, suggests that the results of the 1994 federal, state, and local elections are attributable to general public disgust with government (1995). He believes that educators have been presented with "a unique window of opportunity" to redefine the role of civics in contemporary society. This volume hopes to significantly contribute to the dialogue of renewal.

Our society is facing a variety of complex issues, including a growing gap between the rich and the poor, crime and gangs, a need for a new work force in an advanced technical society, jobs lost to the global market, a weakening of the family, and environmental degradation. Effectively addressing these problems requires a citizenry with a broad understanding of the interdependence of peoples, social institutions, and communities and an enhanced ability both to draw upon and further develop this knowledge as it confronts human problems (Stanton, 1990). Yet, as we face this need, we have a citizenry whose members are isolated from each other and civically disconnected. Government is seen as "alien." The current politically conservative sentiment embodies some of this antigovernment attitude in wanting to severely limit government, reduce taxation, and set term limits. But adopting the draconian measure of having as little government as possible is like destroying a village to save the people. Getting rid of government to remedy its weaknesses also eliminates the very institutions that help us express our democratic purposes.

Taylor (1994) identifies several characteristics of our hypertrophy. This includes the aforementioned alienation from government but also alienation at work. We accept "alienated labor in return for consumer affluence" (p. 65). Another symptom of our hypertrophy is fragmentation of the family, resulting in a lack of a sense of commitment. We also lack control over priorities. We seem to be unable to set long-term environmental goals. A good example of this is the reluctance of the auto industry to create cars that use alternative fuels. As long as the American public demands automobiles that run on fossil fuels, the auto industry will provide these cars and resist attempts to move toward options such as hydrogen cells. Our collective silence on priorities seems to be the condition of our freedom to build our own private spaces and live our own self-contained lives. We are becoming increasingly materialistic. Most important, we seem to have become enmeshed in the ideology of individualism.

According to Bellah and his colleagues, this is to regard the self as the sole reality (Bellah and others, 1985). This view of self stresses the goal of personal fulfillment. Seen from the perspective of the dialectic between our need for a higher sense of purpose and our fears that we may be victimized by rational and technological forces, seeking a deeper sense of self and achieving inner serenity are certainly worthy and understandable—whether through Eastern religions or through reading books such as Moore's *Care of the Soul.*

However, the issue becomes more complex as we become increasingly self-preoccupied to avoid confronting the underlying social sources of our malaise or anomie. This is illustrated by the many talk shows that glorify our innermost private feelings and actions. As an outgrowth of our privatized sense of self, we tend to frame social problems in privatized terms. For example, we blame the poor for poverty and seek privatized solutions for social problems.

Another aspect of self-preoccupation is elitism in government. While complaining mightily about an unresponsive government, we tend to leave government to professionals, while simultaneously setting them up for failure. The failure of President Clinton's attempt to change our health care system can be seen as due to a certain arrogance in the belief that he can "impose" or "sell" needed reforms that must come through grass-roots politics.

Finally, we are morally disengaged. People act as if there are no common moral norms, saying that moral values are relative to each individual or simply a matter of personal preference.

We have a need for civic renewal. Harry Boyte, author of *Commonwealth,* states that "the aim of citizenship is common action on significant public problems, which means the ability to work pragmatically with a variety of others, whether or not one likes them" (Boyte, 1994, p. 65). This is in essence to create what Francis Moore Lappé and Paul Martin Du Bois in *The Quickening of America* (1994) call a "democratic self," the self creatively involved with others. Creating such a self means that we need to recognize our essential sociality, that the self is empty and meaningless without social ties. Meaningful family requires commitment, a meaningful job requires loyalty, a meaningful community requires a willingness to work together with other people on problems of common concern.

Perhaps the biggest problem we confront is that we cannot repair our leaking society by bringing it ashore and plugging the leaks. We cannot dry-dock it. Instead, we must work toward improvement, caulking the leaks while at sea. There are considerable grounds for concern here. With little room for experimentation and the risk that misbegotten efforts will only cause more water to swirl into the boat, we must work steadily but carefully. To stay with the ship metaphor, we must also help our mates adopt new methods of repairing the ship. Instead of trying to fix the broken bilge pump, we may need to lift our buckets one by one in a collective effort to get rid of some of the foul water while we repair the leaks.

Two months before the 1994 elections, the futurist Robert Theobald argued that local communities must develop the ability to select and pursue priorities relevant to them. His rationale is clear: "The failure of current national and multiregional organizations to manage local variations is increasingly glaring" (Theobald, 1994, p. 21). Who or what will serve as the catalyst for renewal? Theobald believes "that the community college should see itself as the heart and brain of its community" (p. 21).

Our task, therefore, is for community colleges to act as catalysts for a national movement of community renewal. There are several specific tasks to be performed. If we are serious about providing our students with the theory and practice of creating and sustaining civic literacy within the polity, what should we be teaching about the nature, meaning, and development of community? And what about the history and character of multiculturalism in America? Finally, what are the responsibilities of individuals in such a society?

Indeed, our community colleges may be our best hope for finding a way to solve our collective problems. The family, church, and local neighborhoods are currently less forceful as mediating institutions, so we place a greater burden on education to respond to our problems. This response requires a unified effort to take on a number of interrelated issues, including promoting a sense of civic responsibility among our students, helping our community renew civic discourse and action, providing human resources to deal with the effects of poverty, and helping create a more democratically minded work force that has the technical skills needed in the twenty-first century.

Amitai Etzioni in *The Spirit of Community* (1993) provides a point of departure. He describes the task in the following manner: "Communities need more people who dedicate more of their time and energy and resources—more of themselves—to the commons. Young people and those who change jobs or retrain will do best if they seek to combine their career with pursuits that are supportive of the community. And the physical environment needs to be designed to be much more community-friendly" (Etzioni, 1993, p. 133). A complex question needs to be posed: What is community and how do community colleges contribute to development?

David Mathews, president of the Kettering Foundation, responds: "I don't simply mean a place or a collection of individuals; I mean a group of diverse people joined in a variety of ways to improve their common well being—a polity" (1993, p. 53). He believes that our nation is experiencing a declining sense of polity. The solution is easy to articulate but difficult to achieve. "Only an engaged public can regenerate a sense of community. The most serious problems facing our communities required the public's active participation. Governments and institutions cannot solve these problems by themselves. If the classic social institutions lack the capability to renew the nation's sense of community, where can we turn?" (1993, p.53).

All of these questions are addressed in the mission statements of many community colleges. What is needed is focus. The chapters in this volume identify empirical models that have begun the process of renewal.

In the first chapter, Lynn Barnett, director of community development at the American Association of Community Colleges (AACC), explains how AACC has come to support service learning, an endeavor that came out of the work of the Commission on the Future of Community Colleges in 1986 and produced a landmark document, *Building Communities: A Vision for a New Century*.

Chapter Two provides an understanding of the need of faculty to make the commitment to developing civic literacy. Leonard F. O'Hara, president of Paducah Community College in Kentucky, provides insight into the creation of an environment of mutual trust and creativity along with an instrument for gauging the level of these factors on campus.

Marietta McCarty, a philosophy instructor at Piedmont Virginia Community College, has attempted to instill democratic values through promoting the curricular integration of ethics and supporting a service learning initiative. She describes the expansion of her service learning efforts in Chapter Three.

In Chapter Four, Robert J. Exley discusses a Miami-Dade Community College initiative, the Partners in Action and Learning project. Reinvigorating individual commitment to community good is a prominent feature in this initiative.

Elizabeth A. Mathias demonstrates how civic literacy can be incorporated into technician education in Chapter Five. She blends a response to the Secretary's Commission for the Acquisition of Necessary Skills (SCANS) with high-tech curriculum support to create the work force for the twenty-first century.

In Chapter Six, C. David Lisman, director of the Community College of Aurora's Community Involvement Program, discusses how the community college's Fund for the Improvement of Post-Secondary Education and its AACC/Kellogg project have led to the creation of a community-development model of service learning.

Nan Ottenritter and Michael H. Parsons describe a ten-year odyssey in which a traditional two-year college seeks to make the transition from a passive, receptive transfer institution to one that is proactive and community engaged. Chapter Seven is an effective case study of the critical incidents in the process of change.

In Chapter Eight, Rosemary Gillett-Karam provides a comprehensive review of the concepts involved in community-based programming. Her focus is on a Kellogg Foundation project that encompasses community colleges in Maryland, Virginia, and North and South Carolina.

Chapter Nine describes the process for integrating service learning into a quality multicultural writing curriculum. Robert W. Franco writes about a program at Kapi'olani Community College in Honolulu, Hawai'i. Franco points out that Native Hawaiians have developed a culture largely shaped by traditional values, ethnic opposition, and economic and political exploitation. They are now actively building their communities and are examining pre-ethnic cultural values to provide direction in this rebuilding.

In the final chapter, Janel Ann Soulé Henriksen provides brief descriptions of programs and research efforts regarding civic literacy. She views this concept in terms of its relationship to issues in our urban society.

References

Bellah, R. N., Madsen, R., Sullivan, W. M., Swidler, A., and Tipton, S. M. *Habits of the Heart: Individualism and Commitment in American Life.* New York: HarperCollins, 1985.

Boyte, H. C. "What is Citizenship Education?" In T. Y. Kupiec (ed.), *Rethinking Tradition: Integrating Service with Academic Study on College Campuses.* Providence, R.I.: Campus Compact, 1994.

Butts, R. F. "Antidote for Antipolitics: A New Text of Civic Instruction." *The Civic Review,* 1995, *8* (1), 20.

Etzioni, A. *The Spirit of Community: Rights, Responsibilities, and the Communitarian Agenda.* New York: Crown, 1993.

Lappé, F. M. and Du Bois, P. M. *The Quickening of America: Rebuilding Our Nation, Remaking Our Lives.* San Francisco: Jossey-Bass, 1994.

Mathews, D. ". . . Afterthoughts." *The Kettering Review,* Summer 1993, p. 53.

Stanton, T. "Liberal Arts, Experiential Learning and Public Service: Necessary Ingredients for Socially Responsible Undergraduate Education." In J. C. Kendall and Associates (eds.), *Combining Service and Learning: A Resource Book for Community and Public Service.* Vol I. Raleigh, N.C.: National Society for Internships and Experiential Education, 1990.

Taylor, C. "The Modern Identity." In M. Daly (ed.), *Communitarianism: A New Public Ethics.* Belmont, Calif.: Wadsworth, 1994.

Theobald, R. "Changing Success Criteria for the 21st Century: What Can Community Colleges Do?" *Community College Journal,* Aug./Sept. 1994, *65* (1), 16–21.

Michael H. Parsons
C. David Lisman
Editors

MICHAEL H. PARSONS is dean of instruction at Hagerstown Junior College in Maryland.

C. DAVID LISMAN is director of the Community Involvement Center at Community College of Aurora in Colorado.

More than any other segment of American higher education,
community colleges play a unique role in their own communities.
The AACC is sponsoring several community-building and service
learning projects at community college campuses across the nation.

Service Learning:
Why Community Colleges?

Lynn Barnett

Community colleges have been at the forefront of the "community-building" movement for a decade. Their mission statements call for them to be community-based organizations, to meet community needs, to provide service to the community. They are, after all, of, by, and for the communities in which they dwell. Today they are being recognized in the service learning field for combining what they do best—teaching, serving, and modeling civic responsibility. More than any other segment of American higher education, community colleges play a unique role in their own communities.

A big push for this agenda occurred in 1986. Responding to four decades of tremendous growth in community colleges at a time of striking demographic changes in the United States, the American Association of Community Colleges (AACC)—the national organization that represents the nation's 1,100 technical, junior, and community colleges—determined that it was time to take stock of the community college movement and develop recommendations to help community colleges move into the twenty-first century with wisdom and vitality. The AACC's board of directors appointed nineteen distinguished Americans to the Commission on the Future of Community Colleges, headed by honorary chair Senator Nancy Kassebaum and working chair Ernest Boyer, chairman of the Carnegie Foundation for the Advancement of Teaching. After eighteen months of study, public hearings, and campus visits, in 1988 the commission released its report, *Building Communities: A Vision for a New Century*. It strongly recommended that "the theme 'Building Communities' become the new rallying point for the community college in America" (Commission on the Future of Community Colleges, 1988, p.11). This theme was to guide the AACC's work for some time to come.

The commission made a point of defining "community." Community was more than a geographic region; it was "a climate to be created," inside and outside the college (Commission on the Future of Community Colleges, 1988, p.11). It recognized the value of diversity and the value of service. One of the report's main recommendations was to establish and maintain strong connections beyond the college. The commission urged "that all community colleges encourage a service program at their institution, one that begins with clearly stated educational objectives," and "that students participating in service programs be asked to write about their experience and to explore with a mentor and fellow students how it is related to what they have been studying in the classroom" (Commission on the Future of Community Colleges, 1988, p.12).

The AACC's president has echoed the sentiments of the commission regarding community-building and service. Supporting community-based programming, he has cited the value of collaborative learning with its high academic standards and spirit of community: "Community colleges are perfectly positioned to be focal points for community-based programs because of their long history of service to populations who have been underserved or poorly served by social programs in the past. . . . Community colleges offer an ideal perspective from which to identify the need for community-based programs and to bring together the individuals, agencies, and organizations that need to be involved in creating them" (Pierce and Green, 1992, p.26, p.27). Further, AACC leadership has challenged its members: "Community colleges, real community colleges, should occupy a special place in their community. . . . They must go beyond . . . especially to developing and building healthy communities . . ." (Pierce, 1993, pp.3–4).

These actions by the AACC coincided with a growing movement that espoused the need for community-building and citizen participation (Barber and Battistoni, 1993; Coles, 1993; Etzioni, 1993; Putnam, 1995; Roueche, Taber, and Roueche, 1995), and with research studies on service learning in higher education (Dutton, 1993; Martin, 1994; Shapiro, 1990; Smith, 1993).

The Community College Community

Representing the largest segment of American higher education, the community college network has the potential for making a major impact on the implementation of service learning across the country. The network comprises 1,100 colleges, with at least one in every congressional district. In the last census of the colleges, nearly six million credit students were enrolled in programs that included general education transfer curricula, technical programs, and specialized training programs often arranged in partnership with local business and industry and with public agencies. In addition, there were more than 5.5 million students enrolled in noncredit offerings, ranging from personal development programs, to English as a Second Language and remediation courses, to high-tech instruction tailored to upgrade specific skills to meet industry needs. Enrollment projections suggest continued increases in the foreseeable future.

The community college student body lends itself to the active nature of the service learning pedagogy. Forty-four percent of students are thirty years or older; most students are employed, 37 percent are part-time and another 29 percent are full-time. Most live in the region served by the college. About 27 percent of the community college student population is minority, a far higher percentage than is reported by other types of postsecondary institutions. More than fifty-eight thousand international students also are enrolled in community colleges. According to 1992 figures, more than half of all postsecondary students with a reported disability attended a community college (Phillippe, 1995). Community colleges are the colleges of choice not only for nontraditional and "second-chance" students seeking associate degrees and specialized training but also for traditional students preparing to transfer to baccalaureate programs. Others return to the community college after attending four-year institutions.

One of the important conclusions to be drawn from this data is that any program targeted to community college students is likely to affect other significant audiences: the workplace, families, and other community groups in which the students participate. Students are local, with strong personal ties to community businesses, organizations, and other residents. They bring what they learn home and to work. The influence of what they learn affects their behavior in their communities. As community stakeholders, community colleges are key players in tackling local problems. In short, community colleges are a natural fit for service learning.

The programs described below feature community-building and service learning; many others concentrated on work force development and other issues.

National Demonstration Programs

As more and more people recognized the mission and capacity of community colleges to contribute to the well-being of their communities, a variety of organizations—philanthropic and government agencies dedicated to the same principles—began to show serious interest in the colleges. With a voice of confidence in the national community college movement, many of these organizations funded three new national AACC initiatives.

AACC/Kellogg Foundation Beacon College Project. During the decade since the Commission on the Future of Community Colleges began its work, the AACC made the notion of community-building a theme for much of its activities and programs. The six-year Beacon College Project was a direct outgrowth of the *Building Communities* report. Generously funded by the W. K. Kellogg Foundation, the project took to heart the commission's challenge to develop programs and services that would build communities. The Beacon College concept required a lead or "beacon" college to form a consortium with at least five associate colleges and then to replicate or implement collectively an exemplary program or service related to recommendations in *Building Communities*. The intent was to use a consortium approach to carry out activities that address the issues identified in the Futures Commission's report to affect communities across the country. The issues were as follows: partnerships for learning, the curriculum from literacy to lifelong learning, the classroom as community, the college as community, connections beyond the college, and leadership for a new century.

A total of twenty-six colleges were awarded two-year grants as Beacon Colleges, selected in national competitions beginning in 1992. Through their outreach, as of spring 1994 the AACC/Kellogg Foundation Beacon College Project had reached more than six hundred institutions and 130,000 individuals. It leveraged more than $5.6 million from other sources. Across the nation, the word "beacon" came to refer to any number of local community-building programs, from student tutoring or student scholar conferences to service learning and civic responsibility (Barnett, 1992).

The Beacon College Project had a significant impact on the conceptualization of later national initiatives, particularly in its emphasis on community-building and collaborative approaches to problem solving. More specifically, the Beacon project at the Community College of Aurora (CCA), "Ethics-Across-the-Curriculum and Civic Responsibility," was the forerunner of the AACC's current service learning initiative. Working with six other community colleges as well as Colorado Campus Compact, CCA implemented a program that included workshops, mentoring teams, and an international conference on faculty development.

AACC Service Learning Colleges Project. In August 1994 the AACC received one of sixty-five grants awarded by the Corporation for National and Community Service (CNCS) as part of the Learn and Serve America program. There were 425 applicants in the nationwide competition.

The AACC's project, "Service Learning and Community Colleges: Building a National Network," got off the ground with additional support from the Kellogg Foundation, the sponsor of the Beacon College Project. The aim of the service learning grant is to strengthen the service learning infrastructure within and across community colleges and to help train faculty in skills needed to implement service learning strategies, including reflection activities. The grant has three components: national data collection, service learning demonstration grants, and technical assistance. The Campus Compact Center for Community Colleges in Arizona is a partner in the project.

Data collection. A recent national survey (Robinson, 1995b) solicited current information from all community colleges across the country to identify programs and resources for service learning. Project staff developed a data base of information collected from more than seven hundred community colleges. Survey results indicate that 75 percent of all community colleges either already are offering some kind of service learning opportunities to their students or are interested in beginning; a full 30 percent reported now offering service learning in a variety of courses. Nearly half of all colleges reported having an office or group that places students in community service opportunities, but only one in five promotes collegewide service programs. Only fifteen colleges reported requiring students to perform community service to graduate; a growing number, however, include participation in service learning on student transcripts. Most service learning programs are quite new, with 75 percent having started since 1990. The survey also yielded more specific information about individual colleges. Thirty-seven percent of community colleges with service learning offer specific, stand-alone courses in community service. Social sciences and humanities courses are more likely to include a service learning component, and most institutions rely on a relatively small number of faculty to implement service learning. Student journals (see Canham, Mason, and Hesse, 1995, for examples) and class discussion appear to be the favorite mechanisms for reflection. Individual faculty members or an administrator with responsibilities for student services are the likely leaders for service learning on a campus.

The four most significant factors in the success of service learning were reported to be, in order, faculty support, administrative support, community support, and student commitment. It is of interest that start-up funding was rated seventh in a list of success factors, above technical assistance, resource materials, and "other." By far, the most frequently cited impediments to implementing service learning activities were insufficient funding (apparently contradicting responses that rated "start-up funding" as only moderately important for success) and insufficient release time. Not unexpectedly, many respondents reported a willingness to share information about their own programs (Robinson and Barnett, in press).

Grants. After a national request-for-proposals competition, a review panel selected eight colleges in December 1994 as the new AACC Service Learning Colleges, each receiving a $12,000 grant for the first year of an expected three-year program. Each college was encouraged to innovate and to adapt their approaches to the special needs of their communities. The grantees submitted action plans to implement programs that address community needs in the areas of education, public safety, human needs, and environmental needs—the areas specified by the CNCS (Robinson, 1995a). The colleges are as follows:

Alpena Community College, Alpena, Michigan. This project provides tutorial assistance to elementary and secondary school students and assists retirement-age citizens.

Flathead Valley Community College, Kalispell, Montana. FVCC has focused its service learning grant activities on a single environmental area: solid waste management and water quality. Its Waste Not Project features strong community agency participation as well as faculty, administrator, and student support.

Hocking Technical College, Nelsonville, Ohio. Hocking is establishing a service learning center and data bank on community needs, and has implemented a faculty orientation program that includes a day of service by faculty.

Johnson County Community College, Overland Park, Kansas. In a wide-ranging effort, JCCC students are providing service to the elderly and to at-risk youth, educating the public on recycling and conservation, and acting as companions for mentally ill individuals.

Kapi'olani Community College, Honolulu, Hawaii. Reflecting its diverse community and student body, KCC emphasizes multiculturalism in its service and learning. Faculty in a variety of disciplines are creating a set of fifteen integrated course offerings with strong service learning components.

Monroe Community College, Rochester, New York. In a unique partnership with the city police department, and with strong support from Blue Cross/Blue Shield in the corporate sector, college students and community residents are engaged in community policing. MCC has benefited from the expertise of a faculty member who is a twenty-year veteran of the police force. The college is looking at ways to expand the service learning experience beyond its criminal justice program.

Prestonsburg Community College, Prestonsburg, Kentucky. Set in rural Appalachia, Prestonsburg is capitalizing on both the strong commitment to and rich opportunities for service in the area. Workshops and training programs with local agencies help strengthen partnerships and highlight placement opportunities, but students often rely on their own intimate knowledge of the community to identify sites for their service.

Truman College, Chicago, Illinois. An inner-city college in the Uptown area of Chicago, Truman has both a highly diverse student population, with students from all over the world, and significant needs within its own walls. The college houses Truman Middle College, an alternative high school for dropouts that is an ideal site for tutoring, mentoring, and other service activities. The service learning leadership team is led by a counselor and includes the chairs of the math, biology, and sociology departments. Community policing and environmental restoration of Illinois' plains areas were the first areas of community service.

All of the colleges are strengthening their local organizational structures, faculty training in reflection activities, and community partnerships to enhance civic responsibility. In the first six months of their grants, the AACC Service Learning Colleges engaged more than seven hundred individuals in service learning, all the while working to get systems in place that would assure program continuance beyond the grant period. Several participant reflection essays suggest the impact of the project after its first year (Brooks, 1995; DiCroce, 1995; Ottenritter, 1995a, 1995b).

With the support of the Kellogg Foundation in the second year of the AACC project, small technical assistance grants were awarded to three additional colleges that fell into institutional categories not previously represented (tribal, Hispanic-serving, and multicampus college). They are Navajo Community College, Tsaile, Arizona; Albuquerque Technical-Vocational Institute, Albuquerque, New Mexico; and Northern Virginia Community College-Manassas, Manassas, Virginia. Regional workshops were part of the second-year plan for the original eight AACC Service Learning Colleges as a way to help faculty at other community colleges implement service learning.

Technical Assistance. This aspect of the project includes a six-person mentor team, start-up and evaluation project meetings with all project participants, the AACC Service Learning Clearinghouse, and a special project listserv on the Internet. (Listservs are automated programs that serve as distribution centers for electronic mail messages.)

The members of the AACC Service Learning Mentor Team, who bring expertise from both academic and student services perspectives, come from the following colleges: Chandler-Gilbert Community College, Chandler, Arizona; Community College of Aurora, Aurora, Colorado; Hagerstown Junior College, Hagerstown, Maryland; Miami-Dade Community College-Medical Center, Miami, Florida; and Piedmont Virginia Community College, Charlottesville, Virginia. Four of the mentors were involved in the Ethics-Across-the-Curriculum Beacon project, which featured service learning and civic responsibility.

The richness of knowledge and skills among the mentor team members contributed significantly to successful start-up activities in the eight AACC Service Learning Colleges. Although each college was assigned a specific mentor to help with action plans and implementation strategies, the mentor team lent its collective expertise to all the colleges and helped the national staff assess the progress of the project overall and at each institution. Miami-Dade, for example, has developed impressive evaluation instruments that can help ensure the academic integrity of service learning programs (Exley, Young, Johnson, and Johnson, 1995). Site visits and regular reporting are key elements as the project continues. The dedicated Internet listserv has facilitated timely communication among project directors, staff, and mentors. The Service Learning Clearinghouse operates as a resource not only for campus project directors and mentors but also for faculty, administrators, and others interested in service learning implementation at community colleges.

Bridges to Healthy Communities Project. The Centers for Disease Control and Prevention (CDC) in September 1995 entered into a cooperative agreement with the AACC to implement a five-year project called "Bridges to Healthy Communities." With appreciation of the power of community colleges to deliver services, the CDC is supporting a service learning project that will focus on the prevention of HIV infection and other serious health problems. Current research suggests that information alone does not appear to be sufficient for promoting or sustaining behavioral changes, and that intervention programs that bring together campus and community may have better results. The service learning approach will foster partnerships between the colleges and their communities, providing students with learning opportunities in the area of health education while also engaging the faculty and others at the college and meeting community needs. Service learning in this case will touch not only individuals but also their environment.

The Bridges project ultimately will involve between two hundred to four hundred community colleges in a Beacon-type approach to program development. Ten demonstration colleges identified in the first year will bring additional colleges into the project in subsequent years. Some of the AACC Service

Learning Colleges in the current Learn and Serve America project will provide technical assistance as the Bridges project gears up.

National Resources Targeted Toward Community Colleges

The Campus Compact Center for Community Colleges and the AACC Service Learning Clearinghouse are two organizations that offer funding to community colleges for service learning projects and provide information, as well as sample materials, on service learning in community colleges. A brief overview of these two organizations is provided.

Campus Compact Center for Community Colleges (CCCCC). This center, devoted solely to community colleges, is a source of information on service learning, and offers funding to community colleges that are members of Campus Compact. Its annual national conference draws more than two hundred community college professionals, including significant numbers of faculty. Located in Mesa, Arizona, CCCCC is supported by the Campus Compact national office in Providence, Rhode Island, the Maricopa Community Colleges System, and Mesa College.

AACC Service Learning Clearinghouse. Established as part of the Learn and Serve America grant from the Corporation for National and Community Service, the AACC's clearinghouse contains information collected in the 1995 national survey on service learning in community colleges, as well as resource lists and sample materials from various service learning practitioners. The clearinghouse can point users to sources of funding or program information, including that from community colleges that have had service learning programs in place for some time, such as Brevard Community College in Florida.

Conclusion

Community colleges are important leaders in the burgeoning service learning movement, and rightly so. The objective of service learning—to integrate service with academic instruction while emphasizing critical reflection and civic responsibility—is a genuine match with the mission of community colleges as teaching and community-serving institutions. Service learning is effective teaching; it is community-building. It is about collaboration and partnerships with community members. Community colleges, which are crucial to the wellness of American communities, can strengthen their ability to serve those communities by implementing service learning programs on their campuses. The American Association of Community Colleges recognizes service learning as a powerful approach to community building. The impact can be limitless.

References

Barber, B. R., and Battistoni, R. M. *Education for Democracy.* Dubuque, Iowa: Kendall/Hunt, 1993.

Barnett, L. (ed.). *Beacon College Project Directory.* Washington, D.C.: American Association of Community Colleges, 1992.

Brooks, S. "To Learn and Serve: Service Learning a Fresh Field for Building Communities." *Community College Times,* 1995, 7 (5), 2, 11.

Canham, J., Mason, M., and Hesse, M. (eds.). *Unspoken.* Chandler, Ariz.: Chandler-Gilbert Community College, 1995.

Coles, R. *The Call of Service: A Witness to Idealism.* Boston: Houghton Mifflin, 1993.

Commission on the Future of Community Colleges. *Building Communities: A Vision for a New Century.* Washington, D.C.: American Association of Community Colleges, 1988. (ED 307 012)

DiCroce, D. "Where Education Meets Democracy." *Community College Times,* 1995, 7 (11), 2, 12.

Dutton, L. R. "An Analysis of Practices in Academic Courses with a Service Learning Component at Institutions of Higher Education." Unpublished doctoral dissertation, University of Missouri-Kansas City, 1993.

Etzioni, A. *The Spirit of Community: Rights, Responsibilities, and the Communitarian Agenda.* New York: Crown, 1993.

Exley, R., Young, J., Johnson, D., and Johnson, S. *Partners in Action and Learning, 1994–1995 Annual Report.* Miami: Miami-Dade Community College, 1995.

Martin, C. "Faculty Perceptions Toward Service Learning Within a Large Public University." Unpublished doctoral dissertation, Pepperdine University, 1994.

Ottenritter, N. "Dear Students." *Community College Times,* 1995a, 7 (5), 2.

Ottenritter, N. "Service Learning by the Book: Six Habits of Highly Effective Service Learning Programs." *Community College Times,* 1995b, 7 (14), 2–3.

Phillippe, K. A. *National Profile of Community Colleges: Trends and Statistics, 1995–1996.* Washington, D.C.: American Association of Community Colleges, 1995.

Pierce, D. R. "The Community College Agenda: A Point of View for the Community, the Community College, and the American Association of Community Colleges." *Community Services Catalyst,* 1993, 23 (2), 3–5.

Pierce, D. R., and Green, M. L. "Community-Based Programming and Diversity." *Community College Review,* 1992, 20 (3), 26–28.

Putnam, R. D. "Bowling Alone: America's Declining Social Capital." *Journal of Democracy,* 1995, 6 (1), 65–78.

Robinson, G. "Eight Colleges Receive Grants." *Community College Times,* 1995a, 7 (1), 1, 8.

Robinson, G. "Going Nationwide: Survey Shows Service Learning Is Catching On, Colleges Either Have Programs or Are Looking to Start." *Community College Times,* 1995b, 7 (8), 6.

Robinson, G., and Barnett, L. *Service Learning in Community Colleges: Where We Are.* Washington, D.C.: American Association of Community Colleges, in press.

Roueche, J. E., Taber, L. S., and Roueche, S. D. *The Company We Keep: Collaboration in the Community College.* Washington, D.C.: American Association of Community Colleges, 1995.

Shapiro, S. J. "Community Service-Learning: A Vital Contribution to Educational Reform." Unpublished master's thesis, Florida International University, 1990.

Smith, M. W. "An Assessment of Intended Outcomes and Perceived Effects of Community Service-Learning Participation for College Students: 'Striking a Chord in the Key of C.'" Unpublished doctoral dissertation, University of Maryland, College Park, 1993.

LYNN BARNETT is director of community development at the American Association of Community Colleges. She is the AACC staff liaison to the National Council on Community Services and Continuing Education, the American Association of Women in Community Colleges, and the National Center for Higher Education Social Action Committee.

To get faculty to welcome and adopt change, colleges must first show
that they understand what faculty value most.

Understanding Faculty Needs:
An Institutional Imperative

Leonard F. O'Hara

Community colleges are places of teaching and learning, and the faculty always
have and presumably long will stand at the heart of that dynamic process.
Those who wish to inject any lasting, meaningful improvement and change
into that electric event must have a clear, even visceral, understanding of and
appreciation for the factors that go into it. In this chapter the reader will discover the core variables that motivate faculty within the work environment.
Fortunately, those variables are both knowable and somewhat controllable.
Moreover, they are few in number, universal in their applicability within academic settings, and commonsense in nature.

Civic literacy proponents, like all crusaders, are likely to be zealots who
clearly see the correctness of their cause and expect it to be readily embraced
and wildly successful. But that simply will not happen in an atmosphere of mis-
trust. Those who would introduce yet another "great cause" into the academic
landscape would do well to first assess the lay of the land. If the extant institutional climate is not good, the venture, no matter how well intended, is almost
certainly destined to failure, or worse, mediocrity. The admonition "Know thy-
self" is very much in order here. If the climate at home, once assessed, is found
to be good, then and only then will faculty and others be excited about adding
yet another layer of external service to their already filled plates.

Herding Cats

"Trying to work with faculty is like herding cats." This one-liner always gets a
good laugh at conferences, especially from administrators, followed by knowing glances and a number of "amens." For those hearing it for the first time, at

least one good anecdote rushes to the lips, occasionally passing the brain first. The metaphor is at once apt and totally off the mark. Anyone who believes that it is usually or mostly true is confusing the *role* of the academic with the academic himself or herself.

It is not the purpose of this work to explore the depths of the role of teachers within a college or university. However, the cat simile breaks down when applied to what faculty want from their work environments. On that score, they are an open book.

As early as 1963, educational researchers were advocating in-depth studies of the environmental factors that lead to high levels of faculty morale in the workplace (Blocker and Richardson, 1963). By that time, the work of Maslow had spawned hundreds of morale, or as this writer chooses to call them, "professional self-esteem" studies. Most of these were done in blue-collar settings; the white-collar professions had come under some scrutiny, but little, if anything, was known about college teachers. Over the past three decades, investigators have asked literally thousands of teachers to name or describe the factors that would lead to high job satisfaction. And they have asked these questions out of more than scientific curiosity. The search for these answers springs from the conviction, born first of intuition and experience and now empirical evidence, that high professional self-esteem is a precursor to high job performance. In education this is an exciting prospect. If taken to its intended logical conclusion, it should lead us to the interface between teacher and learner, the place where the mission of education—that is, teaching-learning—is accomplished.

Occam's Razor

Even the simplest phenomenon produces a dizzying array of variables and data. To intelligently address even a small number of these variables within the space of a chapter or even a major book is difficult. In the case of faculty job satisfaction, it is simply not possible. Fortunately, scientific investigators have provided a solution—Occam's Razor.

Simply stated, this approach requires one to reduce a problem to its core elements. More technically put, Occam's Razor is the maxim stating that assumptions introduced to explain a phenomenon must not be multiplied beyond necessity. Each of us unconsciously applies this technique constantly. Without it, human discourse would be Neanderthalesque at best. A review of the literature on faculty job satisfaction showed that this reductionist approach could be successfully used.

By applying Occam's Razor to the results of the many faculty morale studies, one can reach a reductionist's list of variables that few faculty would, or in practice do, quarrel with. Then by a simple technique—namely, using the short essay and an open-ended question—one can reconstitute the holistic picture of a given institution. The method will be described below, but first, what are the key environmental variables that faculty say can lead to the optimum workplace?

Faculty's Ideal Institution

Can community colleges serve as catalysts for community renewal? Of course—many obviously do. Across the nation these uniquely American inventions proudly proclaim "*Community* is our middle name." Will the civic literacy movement be widely and wildly successful? The answer depends, in large measure, on the extent to which faculty members buy into the concept, embrace it, and ensure its success. And that in turn depends upon the institutional climate within which those teachers work.

"When this nation decides to reaffirm, to empower a teacher and to give a sense of dignity and status [to them], we have in my judgement, found the key to education" (Boyer, 1989, p.9). This statement embodies all one needs to know about faculty professional self-esteem. It is the ultimate in reductionist philosophy. It is all one must understand to effect maximum faculty productivity and, in turn, the highest levels of student success. Unfortunately, it does not tell us quite enough. We must ask for just a little more. Nonetheless, the bottom line in virtually every study of job satisfaction is that employees must believe that they are appreciated, empowered, and valued. There must be a sense of trust between employer and employee that results in workers (in this case faculty) being in control of their own destiny. According to faculty, this type of environment can be created in academe if the administration unwaveringly performs the following actions:

- Genuinely seek faculty opinions and guidance on all matters that touch their professional lives. And do it face to face whenever possible.
- Keep faculty fully informed. Many, if not most, faculty feel that administrators play their cards close to the chest. The feeling that one is on the inside brings a sense of belonging, and with it, power.
- Build a deep sense of trust. This, as stated above, is the most powerful of the variables and encompasses all of the others. It is stated again here because so many faculty list it as one of their key variables. Without trust, the best that administrators can hope for is minimal compliance. Forget innovations, civic or otherwise.
- Remove the mystery or secrecy surrounding the budget process. Faculty have both the need and the right to know how this most controlling of all institutional variables works. They also must be trusted to spend the funds as they see fit, within defined policies and procedures.
- Go beyond academic freedom to the point where faculty have meaningful control over all instructional matters. Next to a deep and abiding trust, this is the most powerful variable in the set. Few things retard self-esteem more than being given an important task and then not being allowed the freedom to do it. Teachers who know they are in control behave accordingly. It is these teachers who will have the self-confidence to empower students. And that is the point of the enterprise. It is the zenith of education itself. Students guided by faculty who know firsthand the exhilaration of empowerment are prepared to enter the civic literacy arena.

- Provide adequate support services. Free teachers to teach and to do the other things that will advance student success. Done correctly, the work of a faculty member is a full-time job.
- Provide ample opportunity for faculty renewal and growth. Most community college faculty rate the intellectual climate of their institution as "fair" or worse (*A Nation Prepared*, 1986). What kind of growth or empowerment can happen in such a climate? As with all professionals, faculty must know that they have a current command of their subject matter. Growth and renewal must be given full berth, whether in the form of training, courses, workshops, research, writing, or things more esoteric. These should be among the very last things cut from budgets, not the first.
- Give faculty a prominent role in institutional goal setting and evaluation. Faculty believe they are significant stakeholders in the enterprise. They want to be involved, and the administration must sincerely invite them to be involved.

We should add one variable to the above list: make an announced institutional commitment to address all of these factors, to make faculty professional self-esteem an institutional priority, and to welcome input of any kind. Then go out and do it. The institution that sincerely and consistently does these things will have created a climate wherein faculty can be the catalysts for their own and their students' civic engagement. The less the college attends to the variables faculty say are important to them, the more likely faculty will be to ignore, resist, or even designate as "just another administrative fad," civic literacy or any other attempt at change. Such teachers are not likely to produce students who wish to go into our communities and help others change their own destiny.

The Fourth Paradigm Governance Model

Something wonderful happened when a research team married the holistic-reductionist approach to institutional practices designed to improve climate and performance—it worked. Not only did the data prove to be astonishingly valid and reliable, but of even greater significance, those being studied applauded the technique's facility for opening up dialogue across the board. Dialogue—real, healthy, deep, constructive dialogue—that unsurpassed precursor to understanding, without which change is unlikely and conflict is all but guaranteed. Presidents, faculty, and site contact persons alike reported insights gained through the application of the technique. The approach is so deceptively simple that it may have to be tried to be believed.

Once the core variables were known, understood, and agreed upon, they were placed in a format that lent itself to transportability—a questionnaire. However, this was no ordinary questionnaire (see Exhibit 2.1 at end of chapter). For one thing, the researcher's need for data was given only minor consideration. Whatever value the investigator would receive from the exercise would have to be incidental, a part of the fallout from the intended benefactors' experience.

Another unique feature of the Fourth Paradigm Governance Model Survey is its brevity. It contains only ten items, the original nine plus one open-ended, "catch anything important that was missed," device that gives faculty a chance to identify institution-specific variables that the nine may have missed.

A third, and arguably the most powerful, characteristic of the instrument is that it allows the subject to explain his or her quantitative responses. This luxury, the qualitative response, is what reestablishes the holistic nature of the data and brings the description of the institution to life. Where the quantitative scores offer little more than the relative position of an institution among its peers, the written comments bring the institution into focus from the faculty perspective. What emerges is a picture that anyone working at the college would recognize. And, from the large number of faculty who chose to write something, it is clear that they welcome the opportunity.

The study instrument has been used three times, in 1990, 1992, and 1994. The 1990 and 1994 investigations will be discussed here. The 1990 investigation involved twenty-five community college campuses ranging geographically from Hawaii to Vermont (O'Hara, 1992). In 1992, several of the original sites were revisited using the same instrument. Then, in 1994, nine campuses within a single statewide system asked to be studied. Figure 2.1 is a graphic representation of the data received by the colleges in the statewide study. The data for Site #33 is broken out separately.

Quantitative Findings

While it was the expressed intention of the investigators to minimize the emphasis placed on quantitative results, these results were nonetheless reassuring. Return rates were high—60 percent and 59 percent in the 1990 and 1994 studies respectively. The validity of the instrument was strong; its reliability was even more impressive.

Validity is defined as an instrument's ability to measure what it claims to measure. The study questionnaire had a built-in checking mechanism. One could examine individual scores on a given item, then compare those scores with what the respondents wrote. Similarly, the institutional mean for a particular item could be compared to the collection of written responses on that item. Low quantitative scores consistently corresponded with negative comments while high scores matched well with faculty's personal opinion of strong institutional performance or effort.

The reliability characteristics proved to be very powerful. Faculty, regardless of locale, repeatedly showed that the questions meant very similar things to them. In 1990, faculty on twenty-two of twenty-four campuses reported that budget matters were the ones over which they had the least amount of control. In the 1994 study, faculty on all nine campuses gave budget matters the lowest scores. It is interesting to note that a low score here did not necessarily

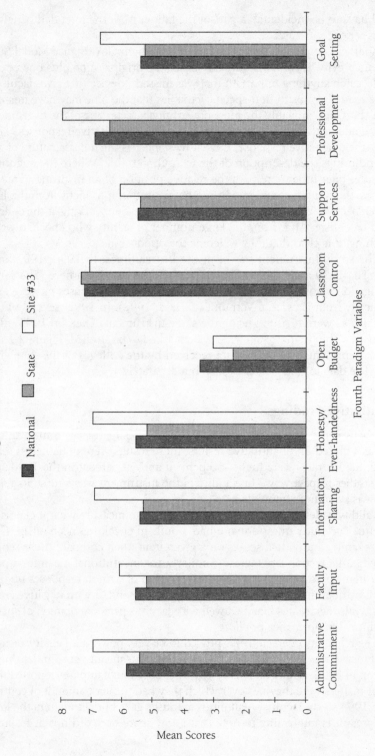

Figure 2.1. Fourth Paradigm Governance Model Variables: Mean Scores, 1994

mean a serious, negative feeling toward the school. When reading faculty comments, it was discovered that many faculty accepted the reality that budget was, for the most part, an administrative matter. Some said that funding was controlled by a state board or state government, thereby precluding significant faculty input.

As for the areas in which faculty perceived that the institution gave them the greatest amount of input or was most sensitive to their needs, the 1990 and 1994 studies were again similar. In 1990, fifteen of twenty-four sites showed that faculty believed they had the greatest amount of influence over "classroom matters," while eight others selected "professional development activities" as being number one. In the 1994 investigation, faculty on seven of the nine campuses chose "classroom control," and the other two put "professional development" at the top of the list.

Institutional Response to the Instrument

All campus CEOs are familiar with the study's report that the process and the results have exerted or have the strong potential of exerting a positive impact on their campuses. A number have asked for follow-up studies, and a few of these have been performed. Several of the campuses have reported that the dialogue generated by the study itself has begun to change the institutional climate. One president said, "Following the administration of the questionnaire and the sharing of results widely throughout the campus, we had the most amiable contract negotiations in our history."

Institutions have used the Fourth Paradigm Governance Model results to establish benchmarks in anticipation of or in follow-up to accreditation visits. Still others have incorporated the quantitative and qualitative results into their long-range strategic planning. Most report that the strongest use of the results is in generating institutional dialogue. "We have disseminated the results to our Board of Trustees," reported one CEO, "and have successfully used the resulting dialogue as a way of instituting campus-wide renewal. The Board got a bird's eye view of the way the institution feels about itself and the problems that it has. We have committed ourselves to solving those problems."

As for faculty, their responses to the nine research variables show that most of their concerns boil down to the impression that the administration is either unaware of or unconcerned with the day-to-day frustrations that teachers experience. This points once again to the issue of trust. This is not to imply that faculty do not raise major issues—they do. But it is the feeling that they are not appreciated or are not treated as professionals that provokes most faculty to say that their campus climate is not responsive.

On virtually every campus, there were sub-rosa issues that this instrument was able to uncover. It then became the responsibility of the CEO who received the results to decide whether or not to address them.

All this is not to say that all campuses found the Fourth Paradigm Governance Model results to be the answer to their prayers. While all presidents did say that the results were useful, a few have made little or no use of them.

One reported that "We simply do not have the time to follow every scent that we get." And more than one president felt that the results, while interesting, might cause campus relationships to deteriorate if openly shared. This situation, too, is one that the administration, in particular the campus president, must handle. It is the objective of the research to improve matters, not make them worse.

If community colleges want to be catalysts in the civic change processes, they would do well to build a storehouse of their own most precious catalyst for positive change—trust. The parallels between this internal action and what faculty and students must do in the civic literacy caldron are unescapable.

Exhibit 2.1. Institutional Ethical Practices and Faculty Professional Self-Esteem Questionnaire

INSTITUTION _____

Introduction:
A significant body of literature suggests that institutional ethical practices affect the professional self-esteem of teachers; further that professional self-esteem affects the quality of the teaching-learning *environment*.

This questionnaire, which is being sent to all full-time faculty at your institution, asks you to judge how well the college performs on nine institutional practices. Question #10 invites you to name another practice that influences the teaching-learning *environment at your college.*

Directions:
Complete the form indicating how well the statement describes or does not describe your institution, place it in the envelope provided, and return it to your college representative (name and location attached). He or she will forward the *unopened* envelopes to the principal investigator. Anonymity will be scrupulously guarded. Thank you.

1. The administration of this college has stated, formally and/or informally, its commitment to promoting the professional self-esteem of the faculty.

0   1   2   3   4   5   6   7   8   9   10

Does not Describe   Describes

Examples: _____

_____

2. Faculty are influential in ensuring that issues which will enhance their professional self-esteem are addressed.

0   1   2   3   4   5   6   7   8   9   10

Does not Describe   Describes

Examples: _____

_____

3. All pertinent information dealing with college issues is openly and freely exchanged.

| 0 | 1 | 2 | 3 | 4 | 5 | 6 | 7 | 8 | 9 | 10 |

Does not Describe   Describes

Examples: _____

_____

4. Faculty are dealt with in an honest and consistent manner.

| 0 | 1 | 2 | 3 | 4 | 5 | 6 | 7 | 8 | 9 | 10 |

Does not Describe   Describes

Examples: _____

_____

5. Faculty have power in determining the institutional budget.

| 0 | 1 | 2 | 3 | 4 | 5 | 6 | 7 | 8 | 9 | 10 |

Does not Describe   Describes

Examples: _____

_____

6. Faculty have control over all appropriate classroom-related matters.

| 0 | 1 | 2 | 3 | 4 | 5 | 6 | 7 | 8 | 9 | 10 |

Does not Describe   Describes

Examples: _____

_____

7. The institution demonstrates sensitivity to the faculty need to devote the proper amount of time and attention to instructional matters.

| 0 | 1 | 2 | 3 | 4 | 5 | 6 | 7 | 8 | 9 | 10 |

Does not Describe   Describes

Examples: _____

_____

8. The institution supports opportunities for faculty professional growth and renewal.

| 0 | 1 | 2 | 3 | 4 | 5 | 6 | 7 | 8 | 9 | 10 |

Does not Describe   Describes

Examples: _____

_____

9. Faculty are meaningfully involved in institutional planning.

| 0 | 1 | 2 | 3 | 4 | 5 | 6 | 7 | 8 | 9 | 10 |

Does not Describe   Describes

Examples: _____

_____

10. List any other institutional variable that is significant to the quality of the teaching-learning environment *at this institution*. Explain.

| 0 | 1 | 2 | 3 | 4 | 5 | 6 | 7 | 8 | 9 | 10 |

Does not Describe   Describes

Examples: _____

_____

References

A Nation Prepared: Teachers for the 21st Century: The Report of the Carnegie Forum on Education and the Economy's Task Force on Teaching as a Profession. Carnegie Forum on Education and the Economy with the Task Force on Teaching as a Profession. Washington, D.C.: The Forum, 1986.

Blocker, C. E., and Richardson, R. C. "Twenty-Five Years of Morale Research: A Critical Review." *The Journal of Educational Sociology,* 1963, *36,* 200–210.

Boyer, E. "Scholars and Mentors." In S. Roueche (ed.), *Celebrations.* Austin, Tex.: The National Institute for Staff and Organizational Development, Jan. 1989.

O'Hara, L. F. "Institutional Ethical Practices and Faculty Professional Self-Esteem Survey Report." *Community/Junior College Quarterly,* 1992, *16,* 319–327.

LEONARD F. O'HARA is president of Paducah Community College, Paducah, Kentucky.

Because societal good depends on the interdependence of its individual members, community service is a unique opportunity to care for yourself and others.

"Love Yourself Enough"

Marietta McCarty

Commitment to service requires a philosophy of service. Why serve? It is so important to ask this question and to continue to ask it. The answers may change and shift in adapting to change, but this fluidity is healthy. Unfounded and ungrounded altruism will wither and be likely to fail in difficult times. What sustains the concept and practice of service is the conviction that service is the right course of action. Why? According to the Dalai Lama, "Only a wise, loving, patient intelligence can create anything that lasts. . . . Only altruism really helps. . . . My definition of altruism is: Be wisely selfish and know that your happiness depends on the happiness of those around you and the world in general. If society suffers you will suffer, so love yourself enough to work for the social good" (1995, p. XIX). In keeping with this quotation, I ask my students what kind of world they want, in what kind of community they want to live. Is it a world in which people are educated, prepared for the workplace, and have their basic needs met? Is it a world in which you feel safe locally and globally? Is it a world in which poverty and violence are controlled by justice and equality? Is it a world in which children laugh and the elderly smile? Is it a world of diversity and unity? Well, here is your opportunity and responsibility. Love yourself enough to work to create this world. This is the mandate to serve. We cannot be happy in the world as it is.

A close look at the nature of democracy is also a part of the philosophical grounding for service. I spend a lot of time talking to students about the theory of democratic rule and what they see in reality today. Do we live in a democracy in the United States today? The key point is that the government was not meant to take care of all our problems, nor can it. Rather than looking within ourselves and joining with our neighbors for solutions and help, we cowardly hand the problems, and our dignity, to the government. Let the government fix our schools, manage health care, regulate and mandate our actions

New Directions for Community Colleges, no. 93, Spring 1996 © Jossey-Bass Publishers 27 for us. Look at our national debt. This abnegation of responsibility has brought us to our knees.

Democracy is meant to be participatory. The government is only one part of a working democracy. Nineteenth-century British philosopher John Stuart Mill speaks prophetically to our age if only we would hear him. In his *On Liberty* ([1859] 1990), Mill repeatedly insists that the size of the government should be as small as possible because individuals can do most things better than a bureaucracy, particularly an unwieldy one. For a democracy to function, its citizens must be educated and tolerant. Without these two characteristics of its people, a democracy can be the worst form of government, warns Mill. The worth of a nation, he concludes, is no more nor less than the worth of the individuals that compose it.

Anna Garlin Spencer in the nineteenth century, and John Dewey in the twentieth, looked at the nature of democracy. Both insist that the people must be actively engaged in a democracy. The government is not the only democratic institution in a healthy society. There must be democratic relationships in homes, schools, places of employment, and between people. This is not to suggest that there be no rules or that there is no authority. It is to suggest that every voice be heard, that citizens act. Recent provocative works propound the participatory nature of democracy as well; for example, Robert Putnam's *Making Democracy Work: Civic Traditions in Modern Italy* (1993) and J. B. Elshtain's *Democracy on Trial* (1995).

With this critical philosophical background, I would like to take a look at four programs that have been born of this examination of service and democracy. In order of their inception as well as of their natural growth and evolution, the programs are Philosophy in the Third Grade, the Summer Program for Inner City Children, Ethics Across the Curriculum, and Service Learning. Our burgeoning service learning program at Piedmont Virginia Community College (PVCC) is the culmination of these efforts, and these continue to reinforce each other in many ways.

Philosophy in the Third Grade

This marks the seventh year of my Philosophy in the Third Grade program. I take the "art of clear thinking" into elementary schools in our service region. I spend at least five sessions at each school, getting to know teachers and administrators, as well as some parents and siblings. These partnerships have proved invaluable in fostering service learning opportunities for my community college students. I have gained an appreciation for the incredible task facing our public school teachers, and this has led me to continue efforts in service learning that target elementary schools specifically. Some of my students accompany me and mix with the children for discussion.

Third grade seems the perfect age for the introduction of critical thinking. I was inspired to do this project for many reasons. I wanted to simplify and learn with the children. I never cease to be saddened at the number of my college students for whom critical thinking is a novel and frightening adventure. This kind of outreach certainly reflects the mission statement of PVCC and, I would think, almost all community colleges. My community college students benefit immensely, and I have new material for the classroom. The college becomes a real presence and source of support for the children and their families.

All participating schools come to the college for the philosophical finale. The children as well as my students have been preparing the one question in their life for which they would most like to have an answer, but the one question seems unanswerable. The children attended one of my philosophy classes, along with their teachers and any interested parents and administrators. My students are stunned, humbled, and encouraged by the shorter philosophers. There is no sharing before the big day of the question, and each child stands and elaborately unravels a worn piece of paper containing the gem. Musings about death and God always top the list. Often people ask me if the children really "do philosophy," whatever that means. Philosophers have dealt perennially with the concepts of time and eternity. Is that not what the children are asking in exploring death and God? I think so. A surprisingly frequent question: "What is nothing?" One child said that if I hadn't given it a name it would not be so hard to answer. On a lighter note, "Why can't I wear high heels?" was also asked, but I suspect there is some philosophy lurking in the question somewhere.

Summer Program for Inner City Children

During the summers of 1990–1994, while I was the director of the Summer Program for Inner City Children, Charlottesville's city council approached me about the possibility of using my third grade philosophy program with city children in the summer. In partnership with our Department of Parks and Recreation, children enrolled in the city summer playground program were eligible to come to the college for "philosophy camp." Children from selected parks were brought by bus to the college for a week's program, and all playgrounds were accommodated in four weeks, two playgrounds attending at the same time.

Buses began to arrive at around 9:30, leaving time for informal games, chat, and settling in until the official start of the day at 10:00. Children were assigned to a group led by a PVCC student, and stayed in that group for the rest of the day. Philosophy was the first activity, with a lot of time for discussion within the small group before the entire group met as a whole. Topics were similar to the third grade topics previously mentioned, and I allowed and encouraged discussion to move to immediately relevant topics for the children: drug use/abuse, violence, personal safety, fear.

After the philosophy session, a variety of activities were available, coordinated to end at noon with lunch on the lawn. Our day ended at 2:00 with talk of the next day's plans. Some activities were everyday options, others were special offerings. Colleagues on the PVCC faculty taught some classes while members of the community volunteered their time and talent for additional opportunities for the children. In offering a job to the PVCC students in this program, I looked for diverse talents, personalities, and backgrounds. Some of the staff were also able to offer sessions in a specialty.

The community college campus is an ideal location for a summer project. There are fewer classes in the summer and the facilities are waiting to be used. Classified staff members also shared talents. Everyday activities included, but were not limited to: art, computer use, fishing, nature trail hiking and flower identification, use of the weight room, street hockey, assorted games, library use, and poetry. Children ranged from six to fourteen years of age, and there was something appropriate for all of them.

What gave my students the desire to work in this program? While there is not just one answer, I think for all of them it was a longing to take philosophical discussion and put it to the test, put theories into practice. John Dewey's pragmatic approach to philosophy was certainly in evidence here: philosophical theories must have practical application and be relevant in a social context.

Aristotle talks about responsibility and free will at great length. We tragically live in a world in which children are killing children. I ask my students where responsibility lies for these killings. If not with the eight-year-old, then with whom? Ultimately, students come to the conclusion that society bears some of this responsibility for creating an environment that fosters violence. Students on the summer staff take this a step further and assume a personal responsibility to address the problem as an individual. They act.

> The basic meaning of compassion is not just a feeling of closeness, or just a feeling of pity. Rather, I think that with genuine compassion we not only feel the pains and sufferings of others but we also have a feeling of determination to overcome that suffering. One aspect of compassion is some kind of determination to overcome that suffering. [Piburn, 1993, p. 109]

When I think of the legacy of this program, I look forward more than I can express to the day that one of these children appears in one of my college classes. Further, I have seen many parents of these children in line waiting to register for classes, often being shown around the campus by the hand-holding child. In the fall of 1995, PVCC has plans to open a "branch" of the campus in the heart of the city so that the college will continue to be a real presence in these lives. I will never know the ways that lives were touched by these four years. There are no meaningful statistics. There were also disappointments and seeming failures. The image I choose to keep in my mind's eye is of the child getting on the bus with a newly potted plant on the Friday afternoon that her week ended. It was a marigold, supplied by a local nursery as a keepsake for each child. The girl turned to her friend and asked what kind of plant this was. Her friend replied, "I think they call them miracles."

Ethics Across the Curriculum

Ethics Across the Curriculum is another PVCC program that has helped pave the way for our service learning initiatives. As a philosophy instructor it is a given that I teach a course in ethics, but ethical concerns are alive and well in all disciplines.

I formed a committee of interested faculty members representing all divisions of the college. This is a key to any enduring program: to target interested people and work with them to get started. Besides teaching faculty I asked a member of Advisement and Counseling to play a major role in these efforts. It has been very effective to have teaching and administrative faculty working together. There are more strengths to draw upon, and differing perspectives. This group became a subcommittee of the Curriculum and Instruction Committee, which gave us an excellent means of communication and visibility.

A variety of faculty made teaching innovations. We looked at ethical issues in the history of the Gilded Age, biology, accounting, nursing, and developmental English. Whereas I actually attended those classes, other faculty became interested when they attended our "brown bag lunches." Faculty would meet in a relaxed, congenial atmosphere to talk about ethics—both in the context of teaching and in terms of ethical concerns at the college. We discussed the awarding of a W grade (withdrawal) when an F grade is warranted, a possible code of ethics for the college, when tutoring help goes too far, and so on. These forums provided an excellent climate for the exchange of ideas, and they have continued with service learning as the focus. Civic responsibility and the nature of democracy will be an ongoing topic.

Service Learning

Although service learning is a national movement with the support of President Clinton, I think we have been moving toward it for years. For me, service learning for my students in the academic year was a natural transition from the Summer Program for Inner City Children. It is the perfect combination of sound teaching pedagogy and meaningful service.

The study of philosophy necessarily provides the intellectual motivation for social action. How can students discuss Platonic justice without taking a soulful look at our own society and world? The need for connectedness is at the heart of the "ethic of care" espoused by such feminist writers as Carol Gilligan (1982), Nel Noddings (1984), and Rita Manning (1992). Gilligan makes us reexamine our approach to the framing of moral dilemmas. Are we asking the right questions? Do we need a different voice? Manning maintains that she has long thought that a soup kitchen or shelter would be the best place to study moral decision making. In Eastern religions the repeated themes of compassion, connectedness, nonviolence, and respect for all life spark a look at one's neighbor.

Along with the syllabus, my students receive a written explanation of service learning on the first day of class, which explains their opportunity. Participation is optional. I recognize that there are many mandated service learning programs across the country, but I have a problem with the paradox of mandated service. Service by definition resists the notion of being forced—either on students or recipients. While clearly distinguished from volunteer work by its emphasis on academic merit, service learning must rely on student appreciation of the call to serve. For some of our students, furthermore, service may take the form of caring for family members or of other avenues that are impossible to anticipate.

Having been given permission by school superintendents to contact elementary school principals, I make the initial contact for my students. Students sometimes choose to return to their own elementary school. Sometimes it is a matter of convenient location. When they leave it up to me, I choose a school based on needs and teachers who have been especially receptive to the service learning agenda. Rather than scattering my students around the service area on an individual basis, I try to concentrate our numbers at specific schools. It is fun for students to work together and share the experience, and the college makes a real impact on life at this one school with a number of students involved. They work at least twenty hours per semester, although most spend considerably more time once they become involved. Even after the class with me has ended, many students continue their service. Students may serve for the sake of the service itself, knowing that it bears directly on the course; or they may write a five-to-seven-page paper "focusing on your look at education today through your experience at the school, with reflection upon any philosophers/theories which are relevant." Whether the student chooses to write a paper or not, I am in constant touch with the service learner in reflecting upon their experience.

Service learning has been a fine chance for students interested in teaching as a vocation to get a firsthand look at education as it is. It is noteworthy that none have been turned off; instead they are more eager to pursue their goal. I think that the transformation of the educational system is critical to our democracy and the individuals who compose it, and students want to be a part of this transformation.

Opportunities for faculty to participate in service learning along with their students are endless. All faculty can take what they teach to schools, with their students, and this also functions as a model for students. Once this is done, the groundwork has been laid for the students' service. Bringing people from the community to the college campus is not difficult and spawns so much good. There are several examples at PVCC. Art students and the instructor work at the alternative high school, and our college art gallery served as the site of the high school's first art show, bringing the high school students and their families and friends to the campus. Advanced accounting students have advertised hours in the central area of the campus to help members of the community with tax preparation. A biology instructor and her students are restoring a wetlands on campus, making a guided trail with identification of wildlife—all open to the community.

Service learning does not require a large amount of money. If a college has it, so much the better. We do what we do with little expense. Big numbers are not important: doing what is done *well* is what matters. There is an investment in time on the part of the faculty member. This is more than compensated for by new energy and assigning a new meaning to education. I have been invigorated by the process as a whole. It is not just the service but the constant evaluation of teaching pedagogy with an open eye.

Conclusion

What better way to conclude than with an excerpt from a student paper relating service to philosophy. This is an Introduction to Philosophy student who served in a rural elementary school.

> Education is the key. With this key what doors will be opened? Will bridges be built? Will communities be salvaged? The challenge has been posed to a new generation, yet the challenge had been extended to the previous generation. What is different now? These questions spark fires within a culture looking for ways to cope with changes that seem to occur at lightning speed. In a time of superhighway communication, technology, and international policy dilemmas, the demand for solutions is pressing on nations and the institutions of family and education. What seems an overwhelming "big picture" must be balanced with the details of how a people can prepare its youth intellectually, physically, emotionally, and spiritually. Aristotle's movie "The End" may have a sequel . . . ["]The Beginning." [Reference to explanation of Aristotle's theory from class lecture.]
>
> Crozet Elementary School has philosophical values that seem to offer this local community a key. The doorway leads their children to a connection with themselves, a sense of local history and preservation, and a yearning to join the larger communities of state, nation, and world. The roots of these values are nurtured in individual classrooms.
>
> [The bulk of the paper follows, with this conclusion.]
>
> Another class became the characters they had read in autobiographies. This multicultural approach was blurring the boundaries of ethnocentrism. One child was a slave and held up the strength of a people in the Underground Railroad. This one experience brought a piece of history previously told only from a white perspective. Their ethnocentrism is becoming school focused rather than race focused. This generation will have never known the burdens of segregation. Yet, they will be taught what price was paid to earn the new privileges. As time marches on they will continue to be exposed to both their history and the ever-evolving issues of our time.
>
> The overall goal of education seems [to be] teaching a virtuous life, teaching responsibility, and teaching freedom of thinking. With their freedom and courage to expand their horizons, they will be better able to contribute to their global community. They will not be afraid to speak their thoughts, challenge an institution, and most importantly, contribute to the building of another bridge. This bridge may lead some on to dream new visions and others will stay to maintain both physical and emotional treasures in the local community. All of them will have been affected in innumerable ways and will long carry their own key. [Laura Weaver Piedmont, 1995]

Yes.

References

Elshtain, J. B. *Democracy on Trial*. New York: Basic Books, 1995.

Gilligan, C. *In a Different Voice: A Psychological Theory and Women's Development*. Cambridge, Mass.:Harvard University Press, 1982.

Lama, D. *Essential Teachings*. Berkeley, Calif.: North Atlantic Books, 1995.

Manning, R. "Just Caring." In E. B. Cole and S. Coultrap-McQuinn (eds.), *Explorations in Feminist Ethics: Theory and Practice*. Bloomington: Indiana University Press, 1992.

Mill, J. S. *On Liberty*. London: J. W. Parker and Son, 1859.

Noddings, N. *Caring: a Feminine Approach to Ethics and Moral Education*. Berkeley: University of California Press, 1984.

Piburn, S. *Dalai Lama: A Policy of Kindness*. New York: Snow Lion, 1993.

Putnam, R. *Making Democracy Work: Civic Traditions in Modern Italy*. Princeton, N.J.: Princeton University Press, 1993.

MARIETTA MCCARTY is instructor of philosophy at Piedmont Virginia Community College in Virginia.

The Partners in Action and Learning project is an example of Miami-Dade Community College's efforts to promote service learning on campus. Results from student satisfaction surveys reveal information on the motives and effects of service learning on students.

Commitment to Community: Service Learning at Miami-Dade Community College

Robert J. Exley

The president of a large university once asked Miami-Dade Community College president Robert H. McCabe what Miami-Dade does. Without hesitation, he answered, "We preserve democracy. We make it possible for thousands of people to gain a college education, people who would otherwise be excluded from higher education, and their education makes it possible for them to become active, committed, and productive citizens." He went on to describe in depth the many accomplishments of the college with regard to its leading the way in providing an open door of access buttressed by a fixed belief in the student's "right to succeed"; however, it is in those first three words—*we preserve democracy*—that he most accurately describes the culture of our college.

We do believe that we are the "people's college" and that we play a vital role in preserving our American way of life, our democracy, and the individual visions of freedom that our country's name evokes for so many. We do believe that every single individual who wants to attend college should have the opportunity to do so, and we couple that with a commitment to providing them the guidance and structure they need not only to attend but also to succeed. If one has any doubt that America remains a place seen by many throughout the world as "the place," we invite you to sit in one of our classes where fifteen countries are represented in a class of thirty students. Come and hear these students describe their personal dreams for the future, or listen to their stories of the family sacrifices that make it possible for them to be here studying at our American college.

NEW DIRECTIONS FOR COMMUNITY COLLEGES, no. 93, Spring 1996   © Jossey-Bass Publishers

Faculty members at Miami-Dade Community College (M-DCC) have been using community service experiences to enhance their courses for over twenty years; however, the past four years have seen a renewed commitment to this teaching pedagogy. A more formalized service learning effort also includes the overt goal of reinvigorating individual commitment to community good. This chapter will provide an overview of how M-DCC now practices service learning, with emphasis on its Partners in Action and Learning project.

Service Learning at Miami-Dade

M-DCC is a large, multicampus, urban community college with five campuses, more than 50,000 students, and nearly 950 full-time faculty members. Miami-Dade County, Florida, provides a rich and diverse setting for the college. Over fifty distinct ethnic groups can be found in the county, and the campuses range from the urban Medical Center Campus, which specializes in health career education, to the Homestead Campus, a rural campus in far south Dade County. The sizes of the campuses range from 1,500 to more than 23,000 students. The student body is a diverse one, with more than 50 percent of the students being classified as nontraditional. The challenges facing our faculty members and students alike are many. However, M-DCC is known as an institution of higher education committed to innovative teaching with a high priority placed on student learning. In short, M-DCC believes in doing what's right to further the education of its students.

Service as a part of different courses is nothing knew at M-DCC. In fact, sixty-five faculty members are listed in a collegewide directory that describes how they utilize service in their courses. Faculty members and students at M-DCC have been involved with our community since the early days of the college and remain involved today. The difference now is that a collegewide effort is underway to determine how best to integrate service learning with a specific focus on civic education into the general education curriculum. The first challenge we faced was to define what we mean by service learning.

David Johnson, in our *Faculty Guide to Service-Learning,* defines *service learning* as "the process of integrating volunteer community service combined with active guided reflection into the curriculum to enhance and enrich student learning of course material" (1995, p. 1). The faculty member uses service as the vehicle for students to reach their academic objectives by integrating teaching objectives with community needs.

At M-DCC, service learning is characterized by three traits. First, service learning demands sound, academically anchored partnerships. The nature of the partnership between the college and any community agency must be based on a shared commitment to the student's education. Second, service learning requires that the service assignments be driven by community needs. It is essential for the community agencies to identify the needs of their constituents as the service opportunities for students. Third, service learning must include a faculty-led reflection component. It is essential that faculty members develop the skills necessary to harvest the learning available through the students' service experience. The most important aspect of a service learning course is the reflection component.

In fact, because community service experiences often produce conflicting emotions and cognitive dissonance in our students, faculty members are presented with rich opportunities to foster student learning. Rogers (1980) writes, "If a person's attitudes toward, reactions to, and feelings about the challenge s/he has experienced are facilitated with support, feedback, and integration, then the probability of achieving accommodation is increased" (pp. 18–19). The support the student receives is key to integrating the experience into the course constructs. With the faculty member's help, each student begins to realize the benefits of service learning as he or she resolves internal conflicts regarding the personal and community issues brought out by the service learning experience. Furthermore, the student begins to comprehend his or her place in the context of community responsibility. For as Silcox (1995) writes, "Meaningful service is not about doing good to someone; it is about the dignity and growth of the giver and the receiver" (p.11). To sum up, service learning at M-DCC requires an active involvement in the learning process from faculty, student, and community members as we connect real-life issues with course theory and context.

Partners in Action and Learning

The Partners in Action and Learning (PAL) project is one of sixty-five initial Learn and Serve America: Higher Education grants funded by the Corporation for National and Community Service, a new government organization created by the National and Community Service Trust Act of 1993. We are now entering the second year of a three-year grant. PAL has three primary goals: (1) to pilot-test campus service learning centers to determine the most efficient means for administrating service learning programs, (2) to provide extensive faculty development on service learning through educational workshops and direct faculty minigrants, and (3) to produce a comprehensive long-term plan for service learning at M-DCC including adoption of college policy and assignment of resources.

The first year of the program resulted in the establishment of two pilot centers (one at the Homestead Campus and the other at the Medical Center Campus), the completion of a successful faculty minigrant project involving sixteen faculty members, and the convening of a college ad hoc committee on service learning under the direction of the college vice president for education. The fall term (September through December 1994) was devoted to educational workshops and finalizing the plans for opening the two pilot sites, and the winter term (January through May 1995) saw the implementation of the minigrants and the opening of the two centers. During this time, more than eighty faculty members attended informational service learning workshops, and fifteen faculty members were awarded minigrants. Finally, the winter term alone saw 755 students under the direction of twenty-six faculty members complete nearly 21,000 hours of service in 145 different agencies throughout Dade County. Every single student received academic credit based on the quality of his or her demonstrated learning.

Analysis of 428 comprehensive student satisfaction surveys reveals some interesting information on the motives and effects of service learning on students. Regarding motivation, the most often reported motivation for becoming involved in service was the gaining of course credit (73 percent, 314 of 428)— in other words, an academic reward for demonstrated learning through the service. The next most often reported motivation items were "the desire to help others" (60 percent, 255 of 428) and the wish for a "new experience" (59 percent, 252 of 428). Of note is that "social concerns" were not a significant motivation for student involvement, with only 28 percent (122 of 428) of the students reporting this item.

However, a comparison of experienced versus nonexperienced service learning students reveals some important differences: the students who remain in service are motivated by the desire to help others (73 percent, 47 of 64) followed by the wish for new knowledge (61 percent, 37 of 64). Also, 39 percent (25 of 64) of the experienced students reported that "social concerns" were a factor. Students who reported that this was their first semester of being involved with service were categorized as "nonexperienced" and all who reported two or more semesters involvement were labeled "experienced."

As for effects, the four effects most often identified by the students were (1) a positive attitude toward community involvement/citizenship (75 percent, 321 of 428), (2) a sense of personal achievement (70 percent, 300 of 428), (3) a sense of social responsibility (69 percent, 297 of 428), and (4) a positive attitude toward experiential programs like this one (67 percent, 286 of 428). It is particularly noteworthy to see that 69 percent of the students reported that they had an increased sense of social responsibility when one recalls that only 29 percent of the students reported "social concerns" as a motivation for involvement. There did not appear to be any appreciable difference for the experienced versus nonexperienced students; however, students in both groups (75 percent for nonexperienced and 77 percent for experienced) reported that their attitude toward citizenship responsibilities was positively affected.

We believe that Partners in Action and Learning is providing us with the kind of information and data necessary to demonstrate that service learning is a vital teaching tool for both enhancing the content of courses and furthering the civic education of our students. We agree with Astin (*Higher Education and the Future of Democracy,* 1994) when he says: "If we genuinely believe that it would be in our own best interest, not to mention the interests of our students and the society that supports us, to embark upon a major effort to introduce a central focus on democracy and citizenship into our curriculum and cocurriculum, we have both the autonomy and the intellectual skill to do it" (p. 26). This is precisely what we are doing through Partners in Action and Learning.

Although PAL involves numerous courses and faculty members, the next section of this chapter describes the course that I teach and how it uses service learning as an essential teaching strategy for addressing one of Etzioni's (1993) basic principles of civic literacy: the pursuit of self-interest balanced by a commitment to community.

Applied Leadership Theory Class

Nowhere will one find more "pursuit of self-interest" than in the highly competitive arena of honors programs. Every honors student receives significant financial support in the form of scholarships and tuition waivers, and in return they are required to complete a core set of honors courses. In addition, every honors student must fulfill a minimum of thirty hours of service to the community for the express purpose of initiating an awareness of one's individual responsibility to the whole. My course is one of the required courses and includes a mandatory service experience.

CLP 2001 is an honors course in leadership that emphasizes understanding of oneself as a unique individual as the basis for developing effective leadership abilities. The main themes include personal assessment, values and expectations, power, motivation, decision making, modeling, and situational leadership. The course addresses the specific leadership skills of planning, organizing, and conducting meetings and presentations. Applied learning experiences are the primary teaching strategies used in the course. The course syllabus states:

> As Honors students, you will be held to a high standard of performance in this class. Also, the only reason that we have class is for you to learn. You are the most important player in this course. My responsibility as your professor is to provide you with the best opportunity for learning that I possibly can. A key to your success in this and future college courses is that you develop the ability and willingness to THINK. What this means is that I hope to use the course materials to challenge you intellectually and affectively. The subject matter of CLP 2001 is based on the everyday conflicts and concerns you and I face in life whenever we attempt to serve as a leader, and we must all deal with these issues in ways that resolve rather than avoid both internal and external conflict.

I utilize two basic texts: *The Leadership Challenge* (Kouzes and Posner, 1987) and *Writing for Change: A Community Reader* (Watters and Ford, 1995), as well as supplemental readings. The first text provides the leadership theories and applied examples. The second text is a service learning reader intended primarily for English and writing courses; however, it contains a superb collection of essays for connecting service to learning. As found in the course syllabus, the course competencies are as follows:

1. *Personality and Self*—you will demonstrate a knowledge of your own personality tendencies and their impact on your leadership effectiveness.
2. *Leadership Components*—you will demonstrate a knowledge of the key aspects for leadership which must be included in your personal leadership strategies and actions.

3. *Leadership Skills*—you will demonstrate knowledge and use of specific leadership skills necessary for serving in a leadership position.
4. *Leadership Responsibilities*—you will demonstrate knowledge of and appreciation for the complexities of individual versus community needs as a leader.

Writing assignments serve as the primary means for evaluating student progress and for facilitating the necessary reflective component. In addition to the writing assignments, various small group assignments and classroom discussions are required of students. The most challenging aspect of the course is to truly connect the service experience to leadership theory in such a manner that the students begin to apply the fundamentals to their own lives and decisions.

Each student is challenged to explore and practice the five basic skills of effective leaders as identified by Kouzes and Posner. Leaders (1) challenge the process, (2) model the way, (3) inspire a shared vision, (4) encourage the heart, and (5) enable others to act. In addition, Gardner's (1987) four moral goals of leadership serve as a basic yardstick for each student to evaluate motives and actions. The moral goals of leadership are (1) releasing human potential, (2) balancing the needs of the individual and the community, (3) defending the fundamental values of the community, and (4) instilling in individuals a sense of initiative and responsibility. This dual emphasis on skills and moral goals results in rich dialogue and serious thought. The student's service placement provides the "real life" setting for the student to both assess the leadership practices of the placement staff and his or her own actions.

Writing assignments make up the bulk of the course's grades. As a part of this course, each student must complete three individual writing assignments, called "feedback reports," in which each student assesses his or her learning to date. Each report is based on a critical discussion question, as follows:

Report I   "What is the leader's responsibility to self and community?"
Report II   "How should a leader use power, motivate followers, facilitate change, and address inequality?"
Report III   "How has your service experience influenced, changed, altered, clarified and/or reinforced your opinions on community and leadership?"

Each student must complete a two-part final examination where he or she describes a "leadership problem" (often this problem scenario is based on the student's service learning experience) and proposes a "theory-based" solution. The final examination includes a written report, an oral presentation, and an oral defense of the proposed solution. The oral presentation and defense occur in the class with class members participating in questioning the proposed solution.

Conclusion

Service learning at Miami-Dade Community College is but one of the examples of how the college is committed to its students and its community. It does, however, provide the most striking example of M-DCC's commitment to making a difference in the lives of our students through focusing on the development of civic literacy. In the context of cognitive development theory, higher education is very good at moving students from the stage of dualism, where knowledge is perceived as either black or white, to that of relativism, where varying opinions and points of view are acknowledged. We in higher education have become quite adept at challenging students' biases, prejudices, and pre-formed values. We can move students along the cognitive development road to the point that they do acknowledge the existence of many questions. What we have failed to do very well is support the students' movement on to the highest level of cognitive development where they make a moral commitment to values and beliefs that are truly the result of their own thinking and processing of varied information. It is only with this type of cognitive development that one can truly devote himself or herself to the betterment of others in true virtue. The ability to be completely devoted to one's own values and principles and yet demonstrate the tolerance of others with differing values only comes with higher-order cognitive development, and service learning provides an extremely effective teaching strategy for this to occur. We at Miami-Dade Community College agree with Martin Luther King Jr.'s comments in *On Being a Good Neighbor* when he said, "One of the great tragedies of man's long trek along the highway of history has been the limiting of neighborly concern to tribe, race, class, or nation" (Barber and Battistoni, 1993, p.557). We are doing everything we can with our service learning activities to extend our concern beyond the traditional limits of an academic institution.

References

Astin, A. W. *Higher Education and the Future of Democracy.* Inaugural lecture presented at the first annual Allan M. Carter Symposium. University of California, Los Angeles. October 26, 1994.

Barber, B. R., and Battistoni, R. M. (eds.). *Education for Democracy.* Dubuque, Iowa: Kendall/Hunt, 1993.

Etzioni, A. *The Spirit of Community: Rights, Responsibilities, and the Communitarian Agenda.* New York: Crown, 1993.

Gardner, J. W. *The Moral Aspect of Leadership: Leadership Papers.* Washington, D.C.: Independent Sector, 1987, pp. 10–18.

Johnson, D. *Faculty Guide to Service-Learning.* Miami-Dade Community College handbook, 1995.

Kouzes, J. M., and Posner, B. Z. *The Leadership Challenge: How to Get Extraordinary Things Done in Organizations.* San Francisco: Jossey-Bass, 1987.

Rogers, R. F. "Theories Underlying Student Development." In Creamer, D. G. (ed.), *Student Development in Higher Education.* Association of College Personnel Administrators, Student Personnel Series, No. 27, (1980) pp. 10–95.

Silcox, H. C. *Motivational Elements in Service Learning: Meaningfulness, Recognition, Celebration and Reflection.* Philadelphia: Brighten Press, 1995.

Watters, A., and Ford, M. *Writing for Change: A Community Reader.* New York: McGraw-Hill, 1995.

ROBERT J. EXLEY is director of the Wellness Institute, Miami-Dade Community College, Medical Center Campus, Miami, Florida.

This chapter focuses on issues related to a new "civic literacy" work force competency by examining some underlying social and technological changes that influenced the creation of the standard. It concludes with a description of a national-level curriculum development and implementation project.

Incorporating Civic Literacy into Technician Education: Why? How?

Elizabeth A. Mathias

Technicians face daily the effects of complex societal and technological change. They use expensive, highly sophisticated equipment, responding quickly to changing customer specifications with the expectation that products are virtually defect-free. Their customers are both internal and external to the enterprise. Technicians work in teams solving complex problems whose solutions often have wide-ranging consequences. An employee's vision and value system can affect team performance.

As the idea of work changed from one of tasks to be performed to one of teams solving problems and appreciating consequences, the need for technicians with civic literacy skills became more apparent. Civic literacy, defined for the high performance workplace, requires employees to have a vision beyond tasks; they must "understand and be able to describe the larger social, political, economic and business systems in which the employee and the firm function" (Packer, 1994, p. 31). This definition came from the work of two national panels that met together in Washington, D.C., in 1993–1994. One panel was convened by the National Association of Manufacturers (NAM), with membership drawn from large and small manufacturing industries or their employee associations. The second panel was of educators drawn from community college system heads or presidents and convened by the American Association of Community Colleges (AACC). In addition to a civic literacy competency, the panels described twenty-one other work force standards. The National Science Foundation (NSF) Advanced Technological Program funded a project to teach some of these competencies.

NEW DIRECTIONS FOR COMMUNITY COLLEGES, no. 93, Spring 1996   © Jossey-Bass Publishers

While civic literacy may well be the most important work force competency community college faculty must teach when preparing technicians, its content may be the most difficult to define. The panels suggested that faculty help students "understand the values that underlie business and personal ethics, government regulation, union-management relationship, environmental and equity concerns, and relationships with the community and its institutions" (Packer, 1994, p.31). By tracing recent social and work force changes and examining academic strategies and courses, insights gleaned can guide administrators and faculty in implementing strategies to help their students achieve this competency.

Change Makes Civic Literacy Preparation Imperative

Change occurred in our economy as our nation lost high-paying, relatively stable manufacturing employment and gained service jobs. Companies forced to stay competitive in an expanded global market changed by identifying core businesses, retraining or trimming employees, and finding more efficient ways of doing business. Meanwhile, the U.S. population became increasingly diverse. People with different beliefs, values, and cultural heritages are being assimilated, and all the while we are learning how to use ever more complicated technology. Instantaneous communications change what we know about life on this earth and how we relate to one another.

Disturbing patterns in our family lives require that our students examine relationships between employment and larger social issues. During one generation, 60 percent of our families saw their incomes decrease. Economic stress drove more women into the marketplace (Swoboda, 1995a, p. 15). Since 1960, the percentage of homes with children that are headed by single parents, mostly women, tripled to 30 percent; out-of-wedlock births went from 5 percent to 29.5 percent (Benson, 1995, p. 47). These statistics portend vast changes in values, with financial and humanitarian implications. Alarming trends require companies to have responsive human resource policies.

If you expect our businesses and industries to be communities where traditions of trust, intimacy, and cooperation are prized, you may be disappointed. Corporations are downsizing. Traditional values underlying employee loyalty change for the survivors as well as for those losing their livelihood. Twenty-five percent of our work force is now labeled "contingent"—part-timers, temporary full-timers, consultants, and contract employees (Swoboda, 1995a, p. 15). Heckscher, interviewing middle managers, found those who "clung to the value of institutional loyalty had relatively few strong ties to institutions outside the corporation" (Hamilton, 1995, p. H5). He argues that the destruction of loyalty related to corporate paternalism is not harmful; in fact, it fosters development of individual capabilities. Loyalty, once thought of as a stable value, has been reevaluated.

Technology and the expansion to a global community has forced America to examine its values and understanding of what citizenship means on a much bigger stage. Multinational companies have outposts around the world. Chuck Zimmerman of Westinghouse Electronics in Linthicum, Maryland, says that with multinational industries, "It's necessary for employees to think about citizenship in a global community." Employees with vision and a greater understanding of interrelationships and causes and effects are essential to sort this out.

Electronic communications are changing our relationships in other ways. We don't have to get out of our homes to tap into "what's happening." David Broder's 1995 editorial highlights an essay by Harvard University professor Robert Putnam titled "Bowling Alone." Putnam is dismayed by the decline of communal participation. Writes Putnam, the depletion in "public capital" (the term he uses to measure the quality of civic life) has been accompanied by a decline in trust in our public institutions and in each other. His conclusion is that "unless more Americans start working with each other on shared civic enterprises, and learning to trust each other, the formal government of this nation will probably lurch from one credibility crisis to the next" (Broder, 1995, p. 8).

Technology and the expansion of a global community have done their share to enhance the value of learning and education. *Workforce 2000,* a research study commissioned by the Department of Labor to furnish basic intelligence on the evolving job market, suggested policy makers find ways to maintain the dynamism of an aging work force; reconcile the conflicting needs of women, work, and families; integrate black and Hispanic workers fully into the economy; and improve the educational preparation of all workers (Johnson and Packer, 1987, p. xiii).

Education is playing a bigger role. The Department of Labor statistics twenty-five years ago showed a male college graduate aged twenty-five to sixty-four and working full time could expect to earn 37 percent more than his counterpart with a high school diploma. Today that differential has doubled to 74 percent (Swoboda, 1995a, p. 15). Quoting Robert Reich, U.S. Secretary of Labor, "Rules have changed. Working hard is not enough; employees can no longer depend on long term relationships with employers. Now you need to make your own way in the economy and learn new skills throughout your career. Insecurity doesn't exactly bring out the spirit of generosity" (Swoboda, 1995b, p. H4).

Society expects educational institutions to have a larger moral dimension. Educated citizens are essential for an effective democratic form of government. Therefore, since values and ethics undergird citizenship, good citizenship requires the ability to think critically and to participate competently. Yet, Morse found that the "words in many mission statements—'to prepare competent and responsible citizens for democratic society'—have lost their emphasis in the curriculum. Higher education must prepare students to be responsible citizens" (1989, p. 26).

How are some colleges and universities confronting the issues of values, ethics, and preparing citizens? What pedagogy encourages student literacy about values, ethics, and appropriate functioning within the broader community framework? What roles are open to community colleges—their trustees, administrators, and faculty? Experienced administrators and educators can offer insights on advancing civic literacy. Some faculty have students confront ethics and values, while others open students to community issues.

Examples of Courses and Pedagogy

Meeting this mission requires courage on the part of faculties. Jim Dollar, assistant dean and chair of the humanities division at Anne Arundel Community College in Arnold, Maryland, says, "Community interests are increasingly pluralistic and expressed through special interest groups. Pressures to influence textbook selections and course content are becoming more common. The message is 'back off' dealing with content values" (personal conversation). Concentrating on process values alone such as listening to others and respecting all individuals does not provide a student with clarification for how such values should be applied. Faculty often focus on individual rights outside of a community context. When education fails to demonstrate to students the reciprocal nature of community obligations, damage is done to the basic fabric of the community.

In Dollar's course, Society and the Individual (Honors 140), students read such authors as Sophocles, Plato, Machiavelli, and Locke. Seminars are used to pose dilemmas to students. Dollar provides as an example, "Locke says God gives us life and property to sustain life; therefore, right to property is unqualified and unrestricted. Two people land on a desert island and decide to divide the island in half. When one of those persons finds the only source of water[,] who owns that source?" In the ensuing discussions, questions surface about dependence on oil, its sources, and the effects of American foreign policy.

The lesson for educators from such simulations is that the world of theory provides good stuff for analyzing real world problems. Dollar has found that if volatile contemporary moral issues are the starting point for class discussions, teachers find themselves faced with students in passionate conflict. The ability to introduce the student to a more analytical approach to such issues is undermined. Use a critical-thinking exercise to move obliquely to newspaper headlines. Don't start with oil shortages.

A team-taught graduate-level course at the Institute for Policy Studies, Johns Hopkins University, offers a model for helping students confront the meaning of citizenship. Robert Seidel, a Johns Hopkins University faculty member, together with a Department of Commerce policy analyst, team-teach Citizenship and the Policy Professional. Seidel recommends blending three concepts for a successful course: the meaning of citizenship, the meaning of community and its interrelationship to the citizen, and a component for service experience. Engagement in community life brings immediate opportunity to examine concepts in action. Students are better able to define citizenship.

A community college example of pedagogy that engages students is provided by professor Steve Ailstock, department head of the Environmental Center, Anne Arundel Community College. He uses applied research for student learning in a county with miles of coastline on the Chesapeake Bay and many tributaries flowing through its boundaries. The Clean Water Act in the mid seventies forced serious efforts to clean up the bay. County executive Robert Pascal selected the community college as a resource for solving county environmental problems. Students develop and plant grasses to save the shoreline, explore and protect wetlands and their wildlife, and work with industry to turn wastelands to parklands.

Ailstock observes that students today need a long-term vision to commit to extended academic study. He believes successful courses depend on teachers making the connections between disciplines and the learner's experiences and life expectations.

Students bring life expectations and experiences that form the basis for their values and ethics to the process of learning. With rapid social change, what students now bring may be inconsistent with the mission and values of an academic institution. If educational institutions need to provide a larger moral dimension to the lives of their students, finding strategies to do so becomes imperative.

A community college model that joins collaboration, connections, and community service is the Center for the Study of Local Issues (CSLI), founded in 1978 at Anne Arundel Community College. This model is derived from a program developed by the U.S. Naval Academy at Annapolis, Maryland to help students confront the meaning of citizenship. Joseph Lamp, a humanities faculty member, pioneered the community partnership concept with a study of the local police department conducted at the request of county officials. Now, 140 to 150 students participate biannually in telephone surveys to county residents asking opinions about issues. Questions are asked about major problems facing residents, their economic outlook, their attitudes toward the news media, and other items. Students learn how citizens feel about various aspects of their community life. Results are shared with county government for management improvement.

Steve Steele, former CSLI director and a social science faculty member, sees the role of the faculty member as facilitator and mentor. He finds this takes time and effort, but in working with students he has come to a clear understanding that "faculty must get in touch with the culture in which our students live[,] . . . that person imbedded in the culture." Major problems with societal and personal relationships "in the lives of our students are more the norm than the exception." He believes faculty should provide modeling for civic literacy but is pessimistic that faculty possess the knowledge or appreciation for such a role. He encounters resistance from faculty to the changing role of the teacher and to the idea of being responsible for making connections for students. The victims are blamed when students fail; he finds little openness to examine the relevance of what is taught.

An example of a community college as a role model for good citizenship comes from the New Hampshire Technical Institute in Concord, New Hampshire. David Miller, professor of electronics/computer engineering technology, teaches an Electronics Project course requiring students to write specifications for, design, and fabricate electronic systems. Successful projects delight nearby scientists at the Mount Washington Observatory, a nonprofit organization that among other things monitors the environment and networks weather information. One student developed a unit used in testing and maintaining remote weather station equipment. Another student developed a prototype wind speed and direction sensor. Civic-minded himself, Miller sees colleges as holders of valuable technical resources having a responsibility to contribute to society's betterment.

What We Have Learned

Ensuring that our students and graduates are competent citizens requires the efforts of institutions: their administrators, faculty, and staff. Boards of trustees and administrators responsible for college operations must provide leadership and demonstrate civic literacy as a value. Faculty too must demonstrate the value of civic literacy.

College boards of trustees and administrators should ensure that they and their college serve as role models to the community. Mission statements publicly express institutional beliefs and drive activities, including the teaching-learning process. Each institution should critically examine what it says about preparing citizens and how its activities support that goal. Link words to actions. Implementation strategies are as follows:

- Collaborate through external partnerships: publicize collaboration efforts promoting civic literacy goals. Collaboration is so important that the Malcolm Baldrige National Quality Award expanded its business award into the education arena as a pilot in 1995 to improve organization performance, facilitate communication, share "best practices," and foster partnerships involving education, business, and the community.
- Educate to systems thinking: systems theory provides a framework for understanding civic literacy goals and organizational interrelationships. Colleges can serve as conveners by offering facilitated seminars to start residents thinking and working together on common issues.
- Lead by example: *The Economist* ("Good Grief," 1995) describes the ethical elements of organizations as extremely fragile. All the pressures in the business world are toward "thinning of the ranks, scrambling for faster decisions and lower costs" (p. 57). Do colleges as businesses have ethics statements formulated and shared?
- Provide incentives encouraging community involvement: support civic literacy behaviors. What role does participation in community activities play in employee performance evaluations? What message does the board and administration send about the relative importance of employee civic literacy activities?
- Provide leadership for collaborative faculty and administrative activities. Mission statements about citizenship preparation are realized in the learning experience.

Faculty members need to do the following:

• Put values "back on the table." Barth (1994, p. 50) writes that "to do less is an abdication of responsibility for our own and for all American children." The Wingspread Group, in *An American Imperative: Higher Expectations for Higher Education* (1993, p. 12), provides a list of questions called "Taking Values Seriously" to serve as a starting point for collegewide dialogues. Answer the question, "What steps will be taken to assure that next year's entering students graduate as individuals of character more sensitive to the needs of community, more competent to contribute to society, more civil in their habits of thought, speech, and action?" *The Civic Arts Review* ("The Missing Piece in the Education Debate," 1992, p. 3) reminds educators that "what is conspicuously missing from [their] debates today is any reference to the civic purposes of education, to education for citizenship. . . . This is the lost horizon of American education. . . . We are missing out on a teachable moment." Begin the discussions now!
• Prepare to confront ethical issues. Faculty members need help to deal with ethical problems that surface during classes. McCormick (1994, p. 159) writes that "faculty need training in ethics . . . at least enough to get by." Become aware of the issues faced by students; listen to ethical dilemmas raised in class. Faculty in the classroom need to recognize when ethical first aid is sufficient or when major surgery is necessary.
• Review syllabi to ensure a balance between individual rights and community responsibilities. Faculty working in teams encourage teaching that builds better connections between disciplines.
• Use the lecture format less; use seminars and experiential learning that involves students in community issues more. A recent study (Frymier and Shulman, 1995) found that communicating relevance builds linkages between content and a student's interest and goals.

The NSF Project Design and Development

The National Science Foundation (NSF) recently funded an innovative national-level community college project to design and test CD-ROM learning modules that integrate elements of the civic literacy competency (among others) into community college general education courses (Packer and Mathias, 1995).

The NSF project employs faculty design teams from five "Lead Colleges" across the nation. Each college represents a consortium of community colleges. Two consortia are state systems, California and New Hampshire; two are industry based, Boeing and the Alliance (of AT&T and its unions); the fifth is the Consortium for Manufacturing Competitiveness. Lead Colleges are Modesto Junior College in California, New Hampshire Technical Institute in New Hampshire, South Seattle Community College in Washington State, Northern Essex Community College in Massachusetts, and Hagerstown Junior College in Maryland.

Five CD-ROM learning modules are being designed by multidiscipline faculty teams with membership drawn from mathematics, science, English, business, and computer information and technology disciplines. Each module will use an actual representative industry problem as a central theme, teach relevant academic content, and require students to work in teams and use technology to create and present viable solutions. Faculty will integrate modules into existing general education coursework, thereby ensuring that students satisfy academic objectives while also achieving a work force competency. Employers will participate in evaluating effects on student achievement. A CD-ROM technology base ensures transportability. Some board members perceive the products as a potential "backbone" for general education.

A national board of directors provides guidance and helps with dissemination. Membership includes representation from the AACC, the NAM, the five consortia, and other industries, including Ford Motors, Focus Hope Project, and the Public Broadcasting System. A steering committee of lead college coordinators, discipline specialists, and industry representatives integrates activities nationally.

Conclusion

Civic literacy, in practice, depends on being able to see the big picture—to look beyond tasks to examine interacting systems and understand cause and effect. Changes have occurred in how we as individuals, the companies in which we work, the environment in which we live, and our global community interact.

Robert Heilbroner (1995) grapples with the effects of progress as a basis for examining possible future scenarios. He sees the only viable solution for our now-global community resting on an historically impotent mass political will. Political processes are gambles on the moral capacities and socioeconomic understandings of the societies from which they emerge.

Education influences our moral capacities and enlarges our socioeconomic understanding. Colleges must form partnerships, use available technology to develop a collective voice, and make preparation of citizen-workers an instructional priority. There may not be many "teachable moments" left.

References

Barth, P. "The Value of Values." *The Education Digest,* Oct. 1994, pp. 49–50.

Benson, P. "Family Patterns Today." *The Education Digest,* Feb. 1995, pp. 47–49.

Broder, D. "This Year, Let's Try to Be Civic-Minded and Civil." *Sunday Capital,* Jan. 1, 1995, p. 10.

Frymier, A. B., and Shulman, G. M. "'What's In It For Me?': Increasing Content Relevance to Enhance Students' Motivation." *Communication Education,* Jan. 1995, *44,* 40–50.

"Good Grief." *The Economist,* Apr. 8, 1995, p. 57.

Hamilton, M. "Learning Something Other Than Blind Loyalty—Author Charles Heckscher Chronicles the Pursuit of a Post-Restructured Middle-Management Ethic." *The Washington Post,* May 21, 1995, p. H5.

Heilbroner, R. *Visions of the Future.* New York: Oxford University Press, 1995.

Johnson, W., and Packer, A. *Workforce 2000: Work and Workers for the 21st Century.* Indianapolis, Ind.: Hudson Institute, 1987.

McCormick, D. "Ethical Problems in Teaching 'Paramedic' Training." *College Teaching,* 1994, 42 (4), 159–160.

"The Missing Piece in the Education Debate." *The Civic Arts Review.* Spring/Summer 1992, p. 3.

Morse, S. *Renewing Civic Capacity: Preparing College Students for Service and Citizenship.* Washington, D.C.: ERIC Clearinghouse on Higher Education, 1989, p. 26.

Packer, A. *An Associate Degree in Higher-Performance Manufacturing.* Report to the Sloan Foundation. Baltimore, Md.: The Institute for Policy Studies, Johns Hopkins University, 1994. (ED 376 894)

Packer, A., and Mathias, E. "Proving a Concept." *Community College Journal,* Oct./Nov. 1995, pp. 38–41.

Swoboda, F. "How the Rules Have Changed." *The Washington Post Magazine,* Apr. 23, 1995a, p. 15.

Swoboda, F. "Robert Reich: The Return of a Policymaker." *The Washington Post,* May 7, 1995b, pp. H1, H4.

Wingspread Group on Higher Education. *An American Imperative: Higher Expectations for Higher Education.* Racine, Wis.: The Johnson Foundation, 1993.

ELIZABETH A. MATHIAS is a principal co-investigator on the NSF grant awarded to the Institute for Policy Studies, Johns Hopkins University, and works at Hagerstown Junior College.

Colleges can engage themselves in community development by providing educational and service learning programs specifically designed to meet local economic and social needs.

The Engaged Campus

C. David Lisman

John L. Goodlad has observed that our school system has often struggled over two philosophies of education, one believing that schools should produce a trained work force, the other that schools should produce competent citizens. Community colleges have attempted to accomplish both objectives, typically promoting citizenship through a humanities core and providing a trained work force through vocational education. However, seldom is there an attempt to proceed in a more systematic way to promote these objectives through engagement with the community. The Community College of Aurora's (CCA) Community Involvement Program (CIP)—supported by President Larry Carter and Don Goodwin, dean of Technology and Community Services and the executive director of the Higher Education and Advanced Technology Center at Lowry (HEAT)—is attempting to bridge this gap. The CIP has grown out of several projects that have drawn the college increasingly into community involvement.

The CIP involves a three-part approach, with a family center providing social support services; a Center for New Work providing a variety of job training programs, including a worker-cooperative development program; and a citizenship initiative helping to provide citizenship and leadership training for area residents. The CIP also houses the service learning program.

Service Learning and Community Engagement

Our service learning program grew out of several grant activities: a Fund for the Improvement of Post-Secondary Education (FIPSE) Curricular Integration of Ethics project (1989–1992), an American Association of Community Colleges (AACC) Kellogg Beacon Civic Responsibility project (1992–1994), and an AACC Corporation for National and Community Service (CNCS) Learn and Serve grant (1994–1996). Each of these projects also have positioned the

 53

Community College of Aurora (CCA) to promote civic development among college students through incorporating ethical and civic deliberation into the reflective components of service learning projects.

Our AACC Civic Responsibility project helped us develop a service learning initiative. A dozen faculty integrated service learning into their courses, and we helped six other community colleges develop curricular integration of ethics and service programs.

Highlights of this initiative included joining the Colorado Campus Compact—part of the national organization that provides service learning resources—in hosting a statewide service learning conference for community colleges. We also co-hosted a forum in September of 1994, entitled "Addressing Community Needs Through Service-Learning and Coalition Building" at Hagerstown Junior College, Hagerstown, Maryland, sponsored by the American Association of Community Colleges and the Kellogg Foundation. This conference focused on the importance of promoting civic literacy through service learning and on the role of the community college in fostering community partnerships.

The service learning program involved thirty-five faculty members who are currently offering service learning in their courses on an average of fourteen courses per semester. The service learning program operates a clearinghouse to assist students and faculty in service placement. Our program has several initiatives.

The service learning program has in place a strong mentoring program with the Aurora public schools, as a result of a two-year Kellogg Grant (1994–1995) for the Aurora Public School/CCA Youth Service Teams project. College students are serving as mentors of Aurora public middle school children, who work together doing community service projects as an intersession activity for two year-round schools. The groups of students do projects at homeless shelters, nursing homes, elementary schools, and the city parks.

Our Kellogg project served as a stimulus for us to become more involved with the Aurora public schools. We teamed with the school district, which received a two-year Learn and Serve grant from the Colorado Department of Education. CCA provides in-service training in service learning for faculty from two middle schools. In addition, the CCA service learning office is providing placement assistance for Aurora public school students.

The CIP's service learning program has been selected as one of four national sites by the Center for Democracy and Citizenship, directed by Dr. Harry Boyte. The Center for Democracy and Citizenship will work with the service learning program to help infuse citizenship training into the service learning program. Six faculty participated in this project during the fall semester of 1995. We are also responsible for providing this same training for the ColordoCorp and helping to disseminate these materials to the AACC Learn and Serve project.

Just as being engaged in service learning has enabled faculty and students to see connections to the community, our involvement in all of these initiatives has helped our college grow in understanding what it means for a community college to be completely engaged with the community.

Community Outreach Initiatives

Our college turned its attention to the development of community outreach programs in the Community Involvement Program. The first issue that caught our attention was that of the homeless in relation to Lowry Air Force Base, scheduled for closure in September 1994. Our president, Larry Carter, had convinced the Cities of Aurora and Denver that a campus should be located at Lowry. During the 1993–94 academic year, CCA and the Colorado Community College and Occupational and Educational System (CCCOES) were negotiating to develop a campus on the 160 acres of the Air Force base that was within the City of Aurora. The other 1640 acres were in the City of Denver. Plans were beginning to form to create a Center for Advanced Technology to be operated by CCCOES. CCA would provide some new advanced technology programs, but other two-year and four-year colleges also would develop programs at Lowry. CCA would offer the general core courses for all of the colleges.

A neighborhood controversy had arisen over a proposal to locate a number of homeless families in two-year transitional housing in vacated Air Force property on the Denver side of the base. This plan could be executed under the McKinney Act, which permits the public conveyance of such property to agencies that provide shelter to the homeless. A number of people in the neighborhoods near the base were opposed to this initiative, fearing that locating homeless families in former Air Force housing would lower property values and bring more crime into an at-risk community that might further deteriorate with the base closure. We began to explore what the college could do to help provide resources for the formerly homeless families and other low-income families in the Lowry community in and around the base.

The Lowry Family Center. We visited a local family center, the Colorado Coalition for the Homeless, and Warren Village, a very successful two-year transitional housing project. I also visited Chemeketa Community College in Salem, Oregon. This college had a program similar to the one we were considering developing at our college. Called the Center for Work and the Family, this program featured a family center and provided training for JOBS clients. (The JOBS program mandates job training for about 20 percent of AFDC clients.) After this visit, our college concluded that we should develop a family center on the future campus.

Our college learned of a statewide family center initiative. As we were opening our campus on Lowry in September 1995, we were able to secure a six-month planning grant. We then received a two-year implementation grant. We opened the Lowry Family Center in March 1996.

The family center, which has a director, a case manager, and a family advocate, provides a variety of resources for families in the Lowry community, including the residents moving to Lowry, the residents surrounding Lowry, and CCA students. The family center offers a variety of workshops to help strengthen families, including GED preparation, parenting, literacy, and youth enrichment classes. The center provides referral services for families in need, including referrals for spouse and child abuse, job training, delinquency prevention, mental health, and substance abuse.

As we were developing the family center, we also began to explore ways that our service learning program could provide assistance to the family center. We developed a paralegal and criminal justice service learning program to serve the family center. Students in these fields provide a hotline at the family center; they also provide basic legal information and informational workshops for the family members.

Center for Workforce Development. With the emergence of the family center, we needed a greater work force development initiative. It was insufficient to provide human resources for low-income individuals. They also needed job training and assistance in getting jobs. There is probably an element of truth in both the conservative and liberal analysis of the welfare issue. Conservatives claim that welfare dependency is the root cause of family disfunctionality and joblessness among people in poverty and looks to set limits on how long people can remain on welfare. Indeed, the current system has many disincentives to getting off welfare, including too few available jobs paying a living wage, people being unprepared for existing jobs, and the high cost of child care.

It may make sense to set a limit on how long people can remain on welfare. But at the same time we need to provide strong human resources for people to help remove personal barriers to transitioning into the work force. The liberal analysis of this problem has an element of truth. As long as people in poverty feel there is no way to get a well-paying job, they have little incentive to get off welfare. We must help such people obtain the job skills that will enable them to secure well-paying jobs. We also need to help people who are underemployed in the service economy get skills that will enable them to move into the technological sector of society, which will provide the majority of the jobs by the year 2000.

No strong program existed at our college for providing low-income individuals with job training. We had relied on the Arapahoe Center for Job Training, our local service delivery area, to provide this job training, and we relied on the Aurora Public Schools' Pickens Technical Center to provide vocational training. However, Pickens Tech provided mainly low-tech training. With plans in place for advanced technical training at Lowry, we needed to develop a strong accelerated skills program. Several programs came about that enabled us to accomplish this. CCA received an Economic Dislocated Worker (EDWAA) grant to provide fast-track training for the first two advanced technology programs at Lowry, metrology and biotechnology. We also received additional funding to expand our Non-Traditional Link (NTL) program, providing skill training for single mothers in nontraditional careers, such as upholstery and auto stereo installation. We then received a Job Training Partnership Act (JTPA) grant from CCCOES to develop a customized fast-track training program for low-income individuals. The NTL and JTPA programs involve providing job readiness and job search training and contracting with companies who receive funding for skill training in return for agreeing to hire individuals in these programs. We also provide the participants an enriched success-at-work course, academic remediation, and job coaching. We have found that companies are much more willing to take on low-income individuals if the individuals receive this kind of support. We are in the process of expanding this program to include fast-track certification programs in such subjects as office software applications and customer service.

These programs are housed in our newly developed Center for Workforce Development. This center not only provides job training for dislocated, displaced, and low-income individuals, but it also will provide career and educational assessment and job placement for the advanced technology programs to be offered at HEAT. These programs will include the following: CCA's metrology, advanced precision measurement technology, and biotechnology programs; Rocky Mountain Manufacturing Academy's metals manufacturing training program and incubator; Pikes Peak Community College's semiconductors program; Red Rocks Community College's automation/robotics program; four Colorado University-Denver engineering programs—the Colorado Engineering Experiment Station with an Expansive Soils Research Center, the Transportation Research Center, and the Bioengineering Laboratory; an educational partnership between HEAT and the Cherry Creek Eaglecrest High School to develop accelerated technical education and/or school-to-work opportunities for Eaglecrest High School students; and the Community College of Denver's dental and health science program. Also, the Colorado Electronic College will provide electronic course delivery, supported by Jones InterCable, for the Colorado Community College system and a portion of Colorado University-Denver's Telemedia Center.

In addition, the Center for Workforce Development is developing a worker-cooperative development program, to be piloted in our Early Childhood Education Program. The purpose of this program is to assist individuals who are working for fairly low wages in child care centers to join together with other child care workers and convert or start up worker-owned day care centers. There is national interest in this as a way to create day care centers that provide high-quality child care. We are receiving grant assistance for this project from Childspace in Philadelphia, directed by Ms. Cindy Coker. As a result of this grant we will become a regional center for Early Childhood Day Care Coop Development. This approach to child care is promising as one of the solutions to the problems of high failure rates of day care centers and poor-quality care. With this model, the workers are the owners. They thus have a stake in the business, making them more committed workers who provide better-quality child care. We plan to provide similar assistance to other businesses, in such fields as home care, hair dressing, custodial services, security services, and manufacturing. We also hope to provide a micro-enterprise development program, currently funded by the Colorado Department of Human Resources, that enables low-income individuals to develop and start their own home-based businesses in a peer-supported environment.

The Center for Workforce Development also plans to coordinate a technological transitions program that will enable people without technical skills to gain math and science training in a laboratory setting. Finally, the Center will serve as the clearinghouse for an urban school-to-work partnership.

Leadership and Citizenship Training. The third leg of our community outreach program is the development of a leadership and citizenship training program for area residents. CCA became involved in the planning process of the Aurora Healthy Communities Project, which met for a year. The purpose of the planning phase was to produce an implementation proposal to the Colorado Trust to create a Healthy Communities initiative in Aurora. After an exhaustive planning process, the citizens participating in this activity received a grant to develop a number of initiatives, including developing a data base of services, an environmental project, and an Aurora Presbyterian project to have a mobile health center. We noticed that nonprofessional residents were underrepresented in the planning process. CCA subsequently proposed that we develop a citizenship training program for all area residents. As a result, we received funding to establish a part-time position for a person to locate potential leaders in the community and to establish a process whereby we can provide leadership and citizenship training for these people. This initiative began in the fall of 1995.

Just as we received word of this grant, we learned that former Kettering program officer Dr. Michael Briand of Trinidad Community College in Colorado, who had established a Community Self-Leadership Project based on the Kettering model, received a CCCOES-sponsored Kellogg grant to spread the Kettering model to other community colleges in Colorado. The Community Self-Leadership model strives to assist college personnel to become proficient in conducting public discussion. Colleges then serve as public sites for members of the community also to become more skilled in engaging in civic discussion and planning. Dr. Briand, interested in the joining with CCA and HEAT, decided to co-locate the Kellogg project at Lowry. We have shared resources to hire a person who can provide leadership and citizenship training. A community-based organizer assists us in locating and recruiting potential community leaders. Our leadership person offers workshops for these new leaders. We hope that this training will contribute to the creation of neighborhood improvement centers and projects and greater grass-roots citizen involvement. We also will provide training for other college personnel in the greater Denver area.

The College Involved in the Community

The combined efforts of the Lowry Family Center, the Center for Workforce Development, and the Leadership and Citizenship program are providing a support system for the Lowry community and the northeastern quadrant of

Denver. These programs in turn will be enriched by our service learning program. The family center will provide human resource support and services. The Center for Workforce Development will provide a menu of job training opportunities that can assist people in entering the work force at more productive levels. The citizenship program will serve to create greater involvement of citizens in finding solutions to their problems. This program is an asset-based approach. Rather than focusing on the problems in the community, the college is attempting to empower citizens to find democratic solutions to the concerns of their community. The citizens, not the college, must arrive at their own decisions concerning their needs and the direction to take. The college can stand ready with human and work force development resources to lend support to the members of the greater community as they begin to develop their considerable untapped resources to find solutions to their problems.

An example of how these programs can be linked together is illustrated by our work with the Rocky Mountain Mutual Housing Association (RMMHA). This nonprofit organization provides affordable rental apartments for occupants who can rent for life at below-market rates (a form of ownership). The apartment complexes are operated by a tenant governance board and provide a day care center. RMMHA already has several of such housing complexes in place.

RMMHA received a HUD YouthBuild grant to provide GED preparation and job training for twenty high school dropouts while paying these participants $7.00 per hour, plus benefits, to help renovate one of their newly acquired apartment buildings. The Center for Workforce Development will serve as the evaluator of this project. Goodwill Industries will provide recruitment and assessment of the YouthBuild participants. Aurora Public Schools (APS) will provide life skill training and a computerized self-paced GED program. Pickens Technical Center will provide on-site job training in their building maintenance program. The participants will work and attend class each for twenty hours a week. Catholic Charities will provide case management. CCA also is offering a citizenship and leadership training component of life skills, and the Lowry Family Center will provide referral services for participants who face serious personal barriers. CCA's service learning office will provide the participants with community service opportunities. APS also will provide the participants with educational and career counseling so that at the end of the project they can move forward with work or educational plans. CCA's Center for New Work also will assist RMMHA in converting this program to a nonprofit company that can continue to do building renovation, possibly retaining some of the youth as employees. We will also explore providing worker-cooperative development for some of these youth in areas such as building and landscape maintenance.

Conclusion

Having indicated how our college's involvement with ethics and service learning has drawn our college into increased involvement in the community through human resource, work force, and citizenship development, I conclude with a few remarks about what all of this may mean for the community college movement.

Most of our mediating institutions, such as our K-12 schools and churches, lack the cohesiveness to help address the economic and social problems that we confront. We have a society of civically disconnected people who see government as something alien to themselves. These people need to come to a renewed understanding of what it means to be a citizen functioning in a democracy. We need not only civic renewal but also a seamless system of human resource assistance, exemplified by CCA's family center, that can provide families in need with counseling, social service referral, GED preparation, and parenting classes. While addressing these needs, we must also create work force development activities that can assist dislocated, displaced, low-income, undertrained, and underemployed individuals. We also need to do this in an educational context that helps our students make good career choices and become more involved in the community. Technical preparation and service learning programs can help accomplish these latter goals. The kinds of programs we are creating at CCA can help significantly extend the role of education in community development. These programs present an image of the engaged community college, which may be our last but brightest hope for systematically addressing the complex social and economic problems with which we are confronted.

C. DAVID LISMAN is director of the Community Involvement Program at the Community College of Aurora in Colorado.

In 1986, Hagerstown Junior College embarked on a ten-year process of renewal. Through community-based programming and the facilitation of community problem solving, the college redefined its civic purpose and formulated and executed an action agenda that will lead the college into the twenty-first century.

In Good Company: A Ten-Year Odyssey in Pursuit of Civic Purpose

Nan Ottenritter, Michael H. Parsons

The 1990s may be categorized as a decade in search of an identity. Most social institutions are experiencing a malaise brought about by eroding or conflicting norms. Higher education has not escaped. Derek Bok, former president of Harvard, reviewed the challenges facing universities, asking, "What have [they] done to respond to social challenge?" His answer, "surprisingly little," is followed by a strong indictment. "Again and again, universities have put a low priority on the very programs and initiatives that are needed most to increase productivity and competitiveness, improve the quality of government, and overcome the problems of illiteracy, miseducation, and unemployment." As a result, they "have accomplished far less than they appear to be capable of achieving" (Bok, 1990, p. 41). Eaton, as vice president for academic achievement and transfer at the American Council on Education, suggests, "We left the [1980s] much as we entered them: we still have serious concerns regarding the context of curricula, student performance, and appropriate pedagogy. . . . But [the decade] did prove valuable: the discussions, the controversies, the challenges produced ten years of sometimes thoughtful consideration of important academic issues" (Eaton, 1991, p. 88).

At the midpoint of the 1990s, a response to Bok's indictment and Eaton's assessment is emerging. A number of scholars have suggested that fostering a nexus between personal achievement and civic and social obligations by students is the paradigm shift facing higher education.

A Twenty-First-Century Paradigm

In Carroll's *Alice in Wonderland*, the Duchess suggests, "Everything's got a moral if only you can find it" (Carroll, [1865] 1960, p. 183). One genre of American higher education lays claim to being "community based." Community colleges, as agents of community renewal, envision the moral as managing change toward an improved quality of life. Parnell suggested that colleges are "examining everything from community leadership to citizen participation . . . in an effort to assess . . . civic health." Colleges then facilitate problem-solving efforts (Parnell, 1990, pp. 187–188).

In 1993, two prominent community college scholars, Lorenzo and Armes-LeCroy, designed a "cascading research" process that produced a new framework based on data from over thirty leaders in higher education. It consists of seven elements:

1. *Think logistically*—envision the dimensions of systemic change; design an institutional culture of responsiveness; focus on systems analysis and integration; develop an "outside-in" priority—community, college, sub-unit, staff.

2. *Streamline organizational design*—increase the pace of institutional decision making; base decisions on empirical data; involve all constituencies in the process; use technology where possible and appropriate.

3. *Reengineer roles and work*—redefine the role of faculty; refocus curriculum on the "outside-in" approach; enhance internal teamwork and external partnerships; modify institutional structure to reinforce new roles and responsibilities.

4. *Diversify funding*—plan and implement "doing more with less"; weave entrepreneurship into the organization's culture; expand philanthropy and partnerships; identify and occupy market niches; implement a "fee for service" process where appropriate; use technology to improve productivity.

5. *Expand options*—focus the educational delivery system on the needs of the customer; tailor programs to meet market needs; establish partnerships for mutual benefit; use technology to serve diverse clients where appropriate.

6. *Assure currency*—teach/train for the knowledge, skills, and attitudes required in the workplace; design curricula for quick adjustments to changing societal needs; focus learning on outcomes; enhance pre- and post-assessment; apply "state-of-the-art" technologies to teaching, training, and curricular needs.

7. *Change success criteria*—focus on "outputs," not "inputs"; design and apply measures of quality; weave "lifelong learning" into the fabric of the college; provide growth opportunities for all members of the college community; develop self-directed individuals and work teams focused on "adding value" to the college's processes and products.

The design is presented as "both a framework and an agent for fundamental change within the community college" (Lorenzo and Armes-LeCroy, 1994, pp. 16–19). Empirically, does the framework produce the desired results?

Hagerstown Junior College (HJC) began the transition from a passive, reactive institution to a proactive agent for community renewal in 1986. The steps taken, thus far, coincide with the framework designed by Lorenzo and Armes-LeCroy. An examination of HJC's ten-year odyssey will lend insight into the nature and success of college involvement in the community to promote civic improvement.

Redefining Civic Purpose

The mid 1980s was a period of profound change for HJC. The college went through a comprehensive reaccreditation in 1984. The reaccreditation team recommended that the faculty and staff reexamine what had been a passive relationship with the community it serves. Two years later the college's president, who had served for thirty-three years, announced his retirement. These changes in what had been a stable organizational culture required a systematic response.

The college administration assembled a multidisciplinary team including faculty, staff, business representatives, government agency personnel, and citizen spokespersons. The team's purpose was consistent with the first element ("think logistically") of the Lorenzo and Armes-LeCroy framework. The group developed a questionnaire to assess the validity of the existing college mission. The instrument was mailed to 580 businesses, industries, and government and social agencies in the college's service area. Three hundred eighty-two, or 66 percent, responded. The planning group reviewed the responses and decided that the college's mission statement and objectives should be revised.

The group chose the educational planning charette as a strategy for gathering data on the dimensions of the revision. A charette is an intensive, outcomes-oriented process that examines needs and possible responses within the total community. Jonsen suggests that three factors make the approach effective.

1. It is "a mechanism designed to integrate understanding about various aspects of the environment, especially as they might be inter-related."
2. It provides "the capacity to translate this integrated understanding into the institution's long-range planning and decision making."
3. It is given "sufficiently high-level priority . . . to ensure its translation into decisions and then implementation" (Jonsen, 1986, p. 16).

All of these factors were helpful as HJC sought to reframe its relationship with the community.

The charette took place in April 1986. Community leaders, educators, citizen stakeholders, politicians, and public service agency staff provided suggestions through a structured, focus-group design. College staff synthesized them into an action plan. The plan was reviewed by selected participants, revised, and finally accepted by the college's board of trustees as a foundation for redefining the college's civic purpose. Faculty, staff, and citizen suggestions and board action are consistent with the third element of the framework ("reengineer roles and work").

The Action Agenda

The major actions emanating from the planning charette have given direction to the management of change at the college. The first one called for the
formation of a leadership council drawn from the college's service area. The
organization was to be composed of business and professional personnel
committed to meeting "the economic, social and educational needs of the
area and enhancing the quality of life for all citizens of the region" (Parsons,
1986, p. 2).

The new president of HJC, appointed in June 1986, took responsibility
for designing the council. On January 27, 1987, the group assembled. For the
past eight-and-one-half years the Greater Hagerstown Committee has provided
direction for the college, the local school system, and county and state politicians in implementing community leadership and lifelong learning, the twin
purposes identified by the charette participants. Specific accomplishments of
the committee include the following:

- Approving the annual and long-range vocational education plans of the col-
  lege and the local school system
- Facilitating the establishment of an upper division and graduate program
  branch of Frostburg State University in Hagerstown
- Sponsoring and participating in the Maryland system's higher education needs
  assessment for western Maryland
- Establishing a manufacturing consortium, Quadtec, to attract new manufacturers and expand existing ones along with facilitating the development of
  HJC's Advanced Technology and Technical Innovation Centers
- Co-sponsoring a joint task force composed of the Economic Development
  Commission, the Chamber of Commerce, and the commercial and industrial
  foundation to assess and enhance the area's business climate. [Meininger,
  1995, pp. 3–4]

The organization continues to direct change in the college's service area. Their
actions contribute to the implementation of the fifth element of the framework
("expand options").

The second action emanated from the recognition that lifelong learning
will be a hallmark of the twenty-first century. Charette participants suggested
that all secondary and postsecondary students be aware of the "real-world"
implications of education and be prepared with the skills and knowledge
needed for success. College faculty and staff accepted the challenge.

In 1988, HJC submitted a grant to the Maryland Humanities Council. The
purpose was to establish a basis for civic dialogue. The grant was approved and
the college sponsored a day-long workshop focused on ethics in the professions. Ninety-five professionals from nine career fields reviewed the status of
ethical practices and presented recommendations for action. The suggestions
emanating from the workshop were published and disseminated to full- and

part-time faculty. They have been applied in a variety of classrooms to enhance the blend of theory and application.

Civic dialogue continues. In 1990 the Maryland Humanities Council funded and the college sponsored a workshop to explore the legal dimension of ethics. In 1992, faculty trained in leadership facilitation under a Phi Theta Kappa/Kellogg Foundation grant involved county employers in the application of leadership principles. In 1994 the college hosted a national conference on the implications of civic literacy for community colleges. In each instance, the results of the activities were disseminated to faculty for use with students. The material emanating from the aforementioned series of workshops is useful in making needed changes. Further, the process of external resource development is based on the fourth element of the framework ("diversify funding").

The third action reinforces comprehensiveness. All students must be prepared for civic leadership. Charette participants encouraged educators to upgrade curricula and teaching skills to ensure that students are ready for the challenges inherent in continuous, multifaceted change. HJC faculty responded enthusiastically to the prospect of developing cultural literacy.

In 1990 the Kellogg Foundation in concert with the community college international honor society, Phi Theta Kappa, designed a leadership development course. The goals of the course are ambitious:

- Provide a basic understanding of leadership and group dynamics.
- Assist participants in developing a personal philosophy of leadership, an awareness of the moral and ethical responsibilities of leadership, and an awareness of one's own ability and style of leadership.
- Provide the opportunity to develop essential leadership skills through study and observation of the application of these skills.
- Encourage participants to develop their leadership potential and to engage in productive leadership behavior. [Feldman, 1991, p. 2]

Faculty endorsed the course as a viable process for facilitating civic leadership. Also, the emphasis on "outputs" and self-directed learning is consistent with the seventh element of the framework ("change success criteria").

HJC applied for and received a grant to train faculty to implement the leadership development course. The first team received training in 1991. They co-taught a credit course and provided training for county employees. Teams have been trained in 1992, 1993, 1994, and 1995. Following training, the faculty member co-teaches with a colleague who has been trained and has taught the course previously. Faculty teaching the course have observed changes in student behavior—including seeking leadership positions, participating in community development activities, and expanding career goals—that suggest civic leaders are being prepared. Further, faculty development is consistent with the sixth element of the framework ("assure currency").

Another strategy for changing faculty and student behavior as well as fostering cultural literacy became available in 1992. The American Association of

Community and Junior Colleges in cooperation with the Kellogg Foundation designed a project to "build communities." They defined community not only as a region to be served but also as a climate to be created. The project was based on the findings of the AACJC commission on the future of community colleges, *Building Communities: A Vision for a New Century.* Selected "Beacon Colleges" had either developed exemplary programs or exemplary services related to recommendations in *Building Communities.* They designed plans to replicate their accomplishments within community colleges that were associates in a consortium.

Hagerstown Junior College became an associate in the consortium assembled by the Community College of Aurora, Colorado. The focus of the consortium was the infusion of civic responsibility into the curriculum. Special attention was given to civic initiatives and student field activities. HJC assembled a planning team composed of faculty, with an administrator as project coordinator.

The purpose of the Beacon consortium seemed to the HJC team to be a logical expansion of cultural literacy. Further, it was an amplification of the Phi Theta Kappa leadership course. Faculty and students involved in civic leadership, civic initiatives, and field activities had ample opportunity to practice leadership techniques. Also, the involvement of college personnel in the community expands the college's civic mission and facilitation of change. The impact is synthesized by Harwood: "When public institutions start to listen differently, they can rebuild their public relationships. But that will require a fundamental shift in approach—from gauging the superficial to listening. It will also require shattering the myth that institutions are now connected to the public" (Harwood, 1995, p. 62).

The planning team participated in a week-long training seminar on the Aurora campus in the summer of 1993. At the beginning of the 1993–94 academic year, the team presented an overview of their experience to the faculty. They suggested that HJC adopt a service learning approach to infusing civic literacy into the curriculum. Service learning is defined as a pedagogy combining community service with academic instruction, focusing on critical, reflective thinking and civic responsibility. The Faculty Assembly and College Council accepted their suggestion, and the college entered the application phase of redefining its civic purpose.

During that same academic year, seven faculty members from the behavioral and social sciences, health sciences, humanities, and engineering and mathematics divisions involved sixty-three students in 892 hours of community service. They worked with agencies ranging from education to social services in the public sector and small businesses to large corporations in the private sector. Service learning was a reality at HJC.

The following year, HJC institutionalized service learning when the College Council gave unanimous approval for the establishment of a service learning advisory board. Members received in-service training and more faculty were recruited, thereby adding to the list of those offering service learning as part of their courses. The council accepted an organizational structure in which a core team of faculty and student services personnel would provide the "hands-on" management of the program, with input and approval from the advisory board. The Beacon consortium, the Phi Theta Kappa leadership development program, and the expanded service learning endeavor have a common element—civic development. Advisory committees and student participants provide information to the council on the impact of the efforts. The resulting data function as a needs assessment, which helps keep the activities consistent with the college's stated purposes. The academic year 1995–96, the third year of institutionalized service learning at HJC, will no doubt see an even greater expansion of service learning and connection of that to other college civic endeavors.

What's Past is Prologue

Academic year 1995–96 begins the last five years of the twentieth century. In preparation for the new century, HJC's president convened a strategic, long-range planning task force, Vision 2000. The group's mission is to assess the college's effectiveness at managing change and to determine the impact of the "repositioning" efforts of the last decade.

The first action taken by Vision 2000 was to sponsor an image analysis. A market research firm is working with college personnel to assess the impact of the college's civic involvement. The analysis is based on the assumption that the college is likely to enjoy a "differential advantage" if its civic endeavors match the requirements of the community that it seeks to serve (Crump, 1994, p. 3).

The process will include a series of focus groups followed by a comprehensive telephone survey. The data gathered will be analyzed and an action plan designed. The steps in the plan will include the following:

- Determining problems, opportunities, and essential tasks
- Designing a commonly held marketing vision for the organization
- Training personnel and implementing essential tasks
- Documenting, monitoring, and adjusting performance to ensure plan implementation

As the action plan becomes operational, tactics that have proven successful in previous civic interactions will be applied.

Another action taking place is the development of a School-to-Careers program, which will support the federal School-to-Work Opportunities Act of 1993. The program is an integrated effort connecting work- and school-based learning. It is a voluntary partnership among secondary and postsecondary educators, local and state employment development personnel, and private-sector employers. College faculty and staff will have the opportunity to focus and expand on the skills developed in previous civic responsibility initiatives.

The steering committee, which is developing the School-to-Careers plan, adopted a vision statement that synthesizes the civic development process. "We believe each student must be offered the opportunity to plan for a successful life. School-to-[Careers] in Washington County is a partnership among students, parents, educators, and employers acknowledging that lifelong learning will produce responsible citizens who demonstrate a strong work ethic and contribute to their community" (School-to-Work Committee, 1995, p. 5). Several community forums have been held, a draft plan is operational, and with the approval of Maryland's state plan, implementation has begun.

The third action that will expand civic involvement is the synthesis of service learning and leadership development. The college will be working with a consortium of other community colleges to expand the outcomes of the Beacon project, focusing on reflective techniques for faculty. The results will be considered as enrichment components for all the degrees and certificates awarded by HJC.

The inclusion process reflects the second element of the framework ("streamline organizational design"). With this activity, the entire system will be operational at HJC. Further, the School-to-Careers program will be used to provide a validation context for the enrichment components. Finally, the ongoing planning and marketing efforts of Vision 2000 will be used to gather data on the effectiveness of these efforts to expand civic development.

Will the changes planned for 1995 and beyond align the college with the challenges of the twenty-first century? It is too early to predict; however, curriculum reform research sponsored by the American Council on Education in 1994 suggests optimism. Dever and Templin Jr. summarize their findings by proposing, "More fruitful efforts are likely to result from applying liberal education models that integrate general education goals, student experiences, and community resources with the aim of preparing citizens to participate effectively in an increasingly complex, rapidly changing society" (Dever and Templin Jr., 1994, p. 34). The HJC paradigm is based on these elements.

Conclusion: The Moral Reexamined

What began as an attempt to structure systemic change has come full circle. The 1986 charette produced recommendations for managing change. The process of implementing them produced profound cultural realignment at HJC.

In 1990, fifteen ethicists, social philosophers, and social scientists led by Amitai Etzioni initiated a social movement called "communitarianism." The purpose of their efforts was to restore community in America through increased emphasis on moral, social, and public order. From a personal perspective, they sought to foster a healthy balance between individual rights and social responsibilities.

Etzioni summarized the communitarian agenda in *The Spirit of Community,* published in 1993. He presents six objectives as the heart of the agenda. Each of them is a useful tool for assessing HJC's progress toward redefining its civic purpose.

1. *Essential moral education—without indoctrination.*   The charette provided insight into the changing requirements of citizens as we enter the twenty-first century. The blending of school-based and work-based education through leadership development and service learning provides students with the skills needed for civic involvement.

2. *Development of community without intragroup hostility.*   The skills imparted to students through the leadership development initiative, their practical application in service learning, and a partnership base drawn from School-to-Careers provides the foundation for community. The involvement of faculty, staff, students, and representatives of public- and private-sector organizations together in developing civic responsibility for the improvement of the quality of life for all meets Etzioni's challenge. "Those most concerned about rights ought to be the first ones to argue for the resumption of responsibilities" (Etzioni, 1993, p. 10).

3. *Increased social responsibility—without the curbing of individual rights.*   The involvement of sixty-three students in 892 hours of voluntary community service creates an enhanced commitment to social responsibility. The emerging sense of community enhances the individual's ability to understand the importance of social responsibility. Also, the HJC image analysis carries forward the charette agenda by identifying new problems, opportunities, and essential tasks.

4. *Pursuit of self-interest—balanced by a commitment to community.*   All of the students who participate in leadership training, service learning, or School-to-Careers activity are receiving degree credit and therefore deriving benefit, tangible and intangible. Their labor enhances community development. From their collective effort will emerge the "commonly held marketing vision" referred to in the image analysis.

5. *Controlling powerful special interest groups—without limiting personal rights of lobbying and petitioning those chosen to govern.*   The model is designed to prepare students to function in the political arena. For example, the strategies contained in the leadership training course prepare faculty and students for effective involvement in the civic arena. The vision for the School-to-Careers program empowers participants to develop the tenets of responsible citizenship.

6. *Affirmation of the public interest—with safeguards of the rights of varied constituencies.*   The purpose of repositioning the college for enhanced civic development is to enhance quality of life, thus serving as an affirmation of the public interest. Concurrently, the voluntary and participatory nature of the activities ensures that varied constituencies will advance their needs while protecting their rights.

Why are these activities compelling in the last half decade of the twentieth century? Futurist Robert Theobald responds: "Decision making requires the consent of the governed to an extent that has never been dreamed of before. This in turn demands that citizens be educated so they can understand the tough decisions we must now make" (Theobald, 1994, p. 19).

Theobald continues his analysis by describing a role for community colleges. "I believe that the community college should see itself as the heart and brain of its community. This is, I am convinced, the approach that could revive the enthusiasm of the community college about the future and provide a worthy challenge for its unique structure" (p. 21).

As the twenty-first century approaches, HJC is in good company: faculty, staff, students, and citizens are poised to work cooperatively to manage change.

References

Bok, D. *Universities and the Future of America*. Durham, N.C.: Duke University Press, 1990.

Carroll, L. *Through the Looking Glass: Alice's Adventures in Wonderland*. New York: New American Library, 1960. (Originally published 1865.)

Crump, R. C. "Marketing and Planning Partnership Proposal." Unpublished report, Markinetics, Inc., August 1994.

Dever, J. T., and Templin, R. G., Jr. "Assuming Leadership: Community Colleges, Curriculum Reform, and Teaching." *Educational Record*, 1994, 75 (1), 32–34.

Eaton, J. S. *The Unfinished Agenda: Higher Education and the 1980's*. New York: American Council on Education/Macmillan, 1991.

Etzioni, A. *The Spirit of Community: Rights, Responsibilities, and the Communitarian Agenda*. New York: Crown, 1993.

Feldman, C. "To Lead or Not to Lead." Jackson, Miss.: Phi Theta Kappa Leadership Development Program, 1991.

Harwood, R. C. "Rebuilding Public Relationships." *The Kettering Review*, Spring 1995, 57–64.

Jonsen, R. W. "The Environmental Context for Postsecondary Education." In P. M. Callan (ed.), *Environmental Scanning for Strategic Leadership*. San Francisco: New Directions for Institutional Research, no. 52. San Francisco: Jossey-Bass, 1986.

Lorenzo, A. L., and Armes-LeCroy, N. "A Framework for Fundamental Change in the Community College." *Community College Journal*, Feb./Mar. 1994, 64 (4), 14–19.

Meininger, H. N. *The Greater Hagerstown Committee: 1994–95 Annual Report*. Hagerstown, Md.: The Greater Hagerstown Committee, 1995.

Parnell, D. *Dateline 2000: The New Higher Education Agenda*. Washington, D.C.: The Community College Press, 1990.

Parsons, M. H. "Charette Action Strategies." Unpublished report to the board of trustees, Hagerstown Junior College, July 29, 1986.

School-to-Work Committee. Unpublished position paper, Washington County, Md., Mar. 1995.

Theobald, R. "Changing Success Criteria for the 21st Century: What Can Community Colleges Do?" *Community College Journal*, Aug./Sept. 1994, 65 (1), 19.

NAN OTTENRITTER is associate professor of human services at Hagerstown Junior College in Maryland.

MICHAEL H. PARSONS is dean of instruction at Hagerstown Junior College in Maryland.

College-community relationships and their civic responsibilities are the focus of this chapter. Examples of collaboration currently in practice will be discussed to demonstrate college-community civic accountability.

Community College–Community Relationships and Civic Accountability

Rosemary Gillett-Karam

Community colleges in America have always had a unique mission, a mission rooted in the democratic tradition of American education. Throughout their history, community colleges, known as the people's colleges, have been sought to respond to ongoing challenges, changes, and dynamics of society. Expected to extend their educational mission externally, community colleges are interconnected with their communities in ways that other higher education institutions are not. Much of their training and coursework is demonstrative of them as monitor or pulsebeat of their communities. If there were such a thing as "grass-roots" higher education, community college education would personify that idea. In short, civic responsibility and strong community relations are the sine qua non of community colleges' existence. Civic accountability, including civic literacy, and its demands for a responsive and responsible society working toward the "common good," is used here to illustrate the concept of collegial-community relations.

Philosophy: Community and The "I-We" Debate

The philosophical roots of community college–community interaction can be found in the debate of social and political philosophers. These thinkers warn of the destructive qualities of individualism carried to its extreme; they see the individual embedded in the social fabric of the community and envision the community as the focal point for shared values. They suggest that responsive communities are those that not only address the needs and beliefs of their citizenry but also those that lay the foundation for voluntary behavior—in other words, civic behavior—to benefit the whole.

Since the founding of this nation, political theorists have questioned the relationship between the individual and the community. In the 1970s and 1980s, this question was extended to inquiry of the culture of America. As Americans celebrated the cult of individualism, its critics were nonetheless aware of growing transitions in our society that questioned the inexorable march of individualism. Leading this criticism were sociologists Robert Bellah and Amitai Etzioni, and philosophers Robert Sandel, Charles McIntyre, and Charles Taylor. Bellah and his colleagues warned, "We are concerned that individualism may have grown cancerous—that it may be destroying those social integuments that Tocqueville saw as moderating its more destructive potentialities, that it may be threatening the survival of freedom itself" (Bellah and others, 1985, p. vii). Another critic, Taylor (1992), pointed to our sense of moral responsibility and shared values toward the public good; he argued for the need to understand the relationship between our private and public lives.

Communitarianism suggests that individuals reexamine their responsibilities to society by moving away from traditional emphasis on individual autonomy and individual rights toward emphasizing their role as citizen and participant in the common good of the community, where shared values develop the good society (Bellah and others, 1991). Citizenship and civic virtue emerge as reminders of the individual's responsibility to community.

The emphasis on common values and commitment to community—in other words, the exercising of virtues to attain good practices in society—according to Bellah and his colleagues (1985) produces the return to America's "habits of the heart" (family life, religious traditions, participation in community) that accrue from American culture, mores, and values. Etzioni (1991), too, suggested that both the individual and the community, in the "I versus We" paradigm, build on the concept of a responsive community, one that appeals to the values members of a community already possess and that encourages citizens to internalize good practices or values they currently do not command. In turn, this behavior would result in voluntary moral affirmation and education for the citizens of a community. The recommitment to community provides a solid foundation for a noncoercive, nondestructive community—where the individual and the community empower one another, where neither is secondary or derivative. Gutmann (1987) suggests that the democratic society (the noncoercive society), broadly conceived, is a good society and thus worth preserving. In a democratic society, members have an effective voice in shaping their institutions. In a coercive society, institutions shape the populace, who has no reciprocal voice.

Etzioni (1993) framed a new moral, social, public order that calls for a reaffirmation of values expressed within the following six guidelines: (1) restoring law and order, (2) saving the family, (3) using the schools to provide moral education, (4) reconstituting communities, (5) increasing our social responsibilities without decreasing individual rights, (6) balancing self-interest with interest in the community, and (7) curbing the excessive power of special interest groups (pp. 1–2). Thus, while Etzioni's early foray into communitarianism was theoretical, his later evaluations of American "community" are contextual and prescriptive. By seeking to impose a national agenda, he removed himself from theory building and epistemology and became an active, accountable voice in the community.

There are other active voices today, some in education. Critical among them are Harlacher (1969); Gleazer (1974); Gollattscheck, Harlacher, Roberts, and Wygal (1976); Myran (1978); and Boone (1992). In particular, these voices extend the idea of community service as a community college responsibility; their voices are deeply embedded in the history of community colleges in America and their commitment to community-based education. These thinkers are concerned with the need to bring community service into the active life of community colleges—to move the college from an internal, "I-based" institution, to an external, "we-based" one.

Education: Community Services and Community-Based Education

Community-based education, initially a community service function that was offered by private and rural colleges as cultural centers for their communities, was adopted by public community colleges in the 1930s (McGuire, 1988, p. 13). After World War II, community services, meaning the voluntary association of college personnel in community functions, became a common role for community colleges; this function quickly expanded to include the following: involving community in program planning, offering college facilities for public functions, and cooperating with community agencies. These were the services Harlacher reported in 1965. Harlacher states, "The scope and effectiveness of the community services provided by the community college determined, to a large degree, the extent to which the community understood and supported the several functions of the community college" (Harlacher, 1965, p. 16). At this time Harlacher defined community services as "educational services . . . above and beyond regularly scheduled classes" and as "serving as a catalyst for community development" (1965, p. 6).

Following this idea, three works were published in 1969, Harlacher's *The Community Dimension of the Community College,* Cohen's *Dateline 1979: Heretical Concepts for the Community College,* and Myran's *Community Services in the Community College.* The concept of community service was broadened to include the concept of the community college working with the community to solve problems. By the early 1970s, two leaders of higher education's national organizations, Alan Pifer and Edmund Gleazer, were discussing the role of community services. Pifer (1974), representing the American Council on Education, suggested that the community college start thinking of itself only secondarily as a part of the higher education system—that its primary role should be that of community leader. Almost simultaneously, the American Association of Community and Junior Colleges (AACJC), through Gleazer, issued a similar statement: "The mission of the AACJC is to provide an organization for national leadership of community-based postsecondary education" (McGuire, 1988, p. 1).

Gleazer's initial enthusiasm for community-based education as "a learner-centered system of lifelong learning committed to the renewal of the community and its citizens" (1974, p. 16) was also discussed in *The Community College: Vision, Values, and Vitality* (1980). For all intents and purposes, Gleazer favored education for direct community development, the expansion of community colleges beyond their role in postsecondary education, and continuing education as the community college's main purpose. Gleazer thought "the community college [wa]s uniquely qualified to become the nexus of a community learning system, relating organizations with educational functions into a complex sufficient to respond to the population's learning needs" (1980, p. 10). It is precisely this point—the movement of the community college beyond its traditional role in postsecondary education—that brought Gleazer and the other writers to a philosophical crossroads. While Gleazer suggested community services as the predominant function of community colleges, others saw community services as only one of the many functions of the comprehensive community college.

Several researchers viewed community-based education as a way to expand education beyond a campus-based orientation to a community-based one (Gollattscheck, Harlacher, Roberts, and Wygal, 1976; Harlacher and Gollattscheck, 1978; Myran, 1978.) Gollattscheck and his colleagues said successful community-based programs demonstrate commitment to the needs of society and work as catalysts to create community renewal of all people and "even perhaps the moral and spiritual renewal of our great nation" (1976, p. 12). Myran (1978) added to his initial concept of expanding the scope of community services beyond degree and certificate programs by expounding on the efforts of extension and adult and continuing education services provided by universities and public schools as a model for community-based education. These were Myran's "antecedents" of community-based education. Harlacher and Gollattscheck (1978) urged community colleges to cooperate with social, governmental, professional, educational, and neighborhood agencies in mutually supportive relationships. Community colleges were asked to cooperate with the community, to serve as catalysts in the renewal of society, to serve as a center for problem solving for community and educational issues, and to become the focal point for improving the quality of life in the inner city. According to the Commission on the Future of Community Colleges in its seminal work, *Building Communities*, "the term community should be defined not only as a region to be served, but also as a climate to be created" (1988, p. 3). Historically, emphasis on community-based education was explained as a link among all community organizations that provided learning activities (Cohen and Brawer, 1991). Throughout the development of these mutually supportive relationships, planning models were emerging. Colleges and communities were influenced by strategic planning and issues programming models.

Strategic Planning and Issues Programming

Strategic planning, a concept developed by business and industry (Drucker, 1980) to demonstrate the inadequacy of long-range planning in a rapidly changing technological environment, was made popular in academia by Keller (1983). Modern strategic planning recognizes that organizations are shaped by outside forces at least as much as by internal ones; it pushes organizations to look beyond their internal frameworks with an eye to "thinking innovatively and acting strategically, with a future in mind" (Keller, 1983, p. 182). Cyert explained that such planning differs from long-range planning in that it places a special emphasis on discerning and understanding potential changes in the external environment: competitive conditions, threats, and opportunities. Strategic planning attempts to develop a greater sensitivity to the changing external world and to assist the organization to thrive by capitalizing on existing strengths (1983, p. vii).

According to Morrison, Renfro, and Boucher (1984), success in planning depends on having an adequate and effective means to identify and forecast what is likely to happen in the external environment and to understand how these events may affect the institution. An environmental scanning model is used to examine the external environment for emerging issues that may pose threats or opportunities for the organization. A committee, composed of an interdisciplinary group, is charged with developing a taxonomy of issues that disciplines the search for important possible developments in the social, economic, political, and technological environments. Such scanning also allows organizations to improve their forecasts of the future (Morrison, Renfro, and Boucher, 1984). Information is gathered, analyzed, and articulated to determine the effects of future conditions on present ones. For example, the following question could be addressed: what should be done now to avoid the catastrophe of violence in higher education? Where long-range planning began with monitoring and moved to forecasting, goal setting, and implementation—more an after-the-fact planning—strategic planning uses environmental scanning to begin the process of evaluation and ranking of issues. Once issues are ranked, coalitions begin their work of designing programs to relieve or resolve the issues.

Strategic planning, therefore, includes information about the changing external environment not usually taken into account in most long-range planning. Strategic planning, guided by environmental scanning, recognizes emerging issues that may pose threats or provide opportunities, and can monitor or identify areas for additional and continued scanning. In a document published by the American Association of Community Colleges, McClenney, LeCroy, and LeCroy use strategic planning to develop the idea of building communities. Strategic planning "emphasize[s] the nurturing or development of those qualities and capacities that characterize community: A concern for the whole, for integration and collaboration, for openness and integrity, and for inclusiveness and self-renewal" (1991, p. 1). The planning process of the community college is integrated with the planning process of the community. This process is a continuous one, shaped by external conditions and guided by the internal characteristics and values of the community college.

Issues programming reflects the importance of a community group that has worked to enumerate and rank "identified issues" that frame responses to issue resolution. The term *issues programming* was coined in response to cooperative extension services' (the responsibility of the Colleges of Agriculture) need to reflect modern changes in agriculture in America. Issues programming is a reaction to traditional patterns of "discipline" programming that purports to solve problems independently of issue identification and resolution.

Similar to strategic planning, issues programming was a concept first used by business. Unlike business, however, cooperative extension divisions employed the concept by attaching it to the concept of program development espoused by Boyle (1981) and Boone (1985). Emphasis is placed on developing programs to achieve economic, environmental, and social change, and the needs and concerns of indigenous or target populations are stressed. Issues are defined as matters of wide public concern that arise from complex human problems (Dalgaard and others, 1988). Issues programming is in contrast to discipline programming, in which a discipline identifies itself with a portion of the public and aligns itself with the specialized concerns of that audience, usually confining itself to a particular method of program delivery. Home economics, 4-H clubs, and farm visits represent the traditional core of extension's discipline programs and efforts at programming.

These concepts—the philosophy of communitarianism, the history of community-service education, and strategic planning and issues resolution—are incorporated into the ideas of community-based programming. The catalytic leadership of community-based programming falls to the community college. It is an idea that extends the community college outward and makes it an active participant in its community; community-based programming also extends the community college's democratic and educational mission to those publics most in need of its aid. Community-based programming activates the concept of self-help and cooperation among community agencies and around identified common needs and the issues that most concern the community and its quality of life.

The Community-Based Programming Model

As a process, community-based programming involves a series of tasks, or goals, that facilitate the active role of the community college as the leader in a responsive community—one that seeks not only to identify the issues that affect the quality of life of its citizenry but also one that is dynamic in seeking resolution of those issues through citizen and organizational cooperation, collaboration, and involvement. Community-based programming includes the following ideas:

- It requires initial commitment by college leaders and trustees as to its importance through inclusion in the college mission statement.
- It scans and examines the community college's environment and publics to determine and prioritize critical community issues—an environmental scanning team is named.
- It posits the community college as the leader/catalyst for facilitating collaboration among diverse groups in the community who form work coalitions.
- It suggests that people who are or will be affected by the issue (target publics, stakeholders, formal and informal leaders) must have direct input into the formal planning model.
- It is responsible for formulating a dynamic plan of action that is designed and implemented for issue resolution.
- It requires ongoing evaluation, reexamination, and monitoring of the action plan.
- It allows new issues to be introduced—the process is a continuous one.

Community-based programming is a model specifically designed to facilitate the community college's role as a leader and catalyst in addressing issue-specific needs in its community. Community-based programming is also systemic. It involves inputs, processes, and outputs. Inputs include assessment and examination of an organization's mission, philosophy, and basic assumptions of its community-based educational purpose(s). By following the community-based programming model, the community college and community organizations can collaboratively move from information and data collection to an activity in which a scanning committee investigates the external environment for emerging issues that may pose threats or provide opportunities to the community. The most critical issues are prioritized for immediate attention and action.

After scanning comes the critical task of identifying the various groups that are involved in these emerging issues. The target public is the most critical of the groups to be identified, because it is this group that has been most ignored by decision makers and among whom the greatest changes will occur. While group theory might suggest that group inclusion in decision making should include all affected groups and all groups crucial to the solution, the common practice is for formal leaders and stakeholders to make the preponderant decisions. Community-based programming expects all groups to be included in decision making; therefore, group development, consensus building, and collaboration are central to it—coalitions are formed around the resolution of issues.

A common vision means consensus on desired outcomes that guide collaborative planning. Once parties achieve consensus through issues deliberation, planning can be implemented. A design for short-term and long-term use can be adopted by the group. The group then is responsible for monitoring, evaluating, modifying, and reevaluating the plan of action. Finally, outputs can be measured, including the community college's ability and success as leader-catalyst in effecting community change and the ability of an educational institution to act as a vehicle for reform in society. Institutionalization of the community-based programming model is expected, and the college-community relation remains continuous.

Figure 8.1 illustrates the major ideas of the community-based programming model. The circular nature of the model suggests that even if an organization enters the model at points other than at the examination of its mission—and, no doubt, many do—this model offers a rational process for reexamining the direction of the organization's issues and programs.

Examples of College-Community Relationships

James Sprunt Community College (JSCC) is a rural community college located in Kenansville, North Carolina. Swine production and tobacco are the mainstays of this agricultural community. JSCC is also one of the pilot colleges of North Carolina State University's (NCSU) Kellogg Foundation—funded project ACCLAIM. Beginning in 1992, NCSU and its cohort of community college

Figure 8.1. Community-Based Programming

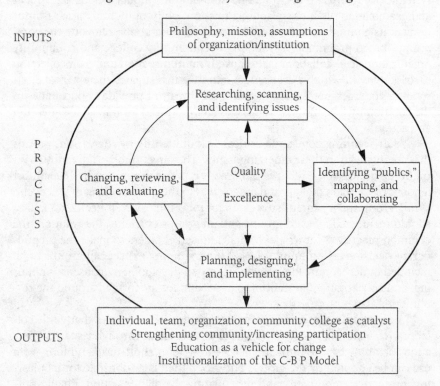

Source: Designed by author for ACCLAIM Project.

professors began training in community-based programming. Formal training lasted two years; during that time three different groups from the college were trained to apply community-based programming in their community. Initially, the college and its leaders—the president, his executive team, and board of trustees—were joined by community leaders (from community agencies) to formally train and learn about the need for and use of community-based programming in their own environment. Don Reichard, president of JSCC, recalls, "Prior to our involvement in ACCLAIM, our knowledge of the external environment in which we operated was limited; we recognized our need to increase our knowledge and understanding of the environment and we were eager to begin to study and learn about the needs of our community" (personal conversation).

JSCC was committed to integrating the community-based programming concept into the mission statement of the college. Officially, JSCC began its formal relationship to its community by adopting its own Philosophy of Community-Based Programming:

Community-based programming is defined as "a cooperative process that involves a series of processual tasks in which the community college serves as the leader and catalyst in effecting collaboration among the people, their leaders, and other community-based organizations and agencies within its service areas in identifying and seeking resolution to major issues that are of critical concern to the community and its people" (Boone, 1992, p. 2). Community-based programming is a key aspect of the JSCC philosophy as a community-based institution and is reflected in the institution's Goal Five, where the college is identified as a catalyst for positive change within the county. Additionally, the JSCC Goals One through Four, which deal with instructional programs, are also to be accomplished as a cooperative process in a manner conducive to community-based programming (College Council Meeting, 1993).

After formally committing to a planned community college–community relationship, the next task is to establish an environmental scanning committee of college and community participants who take responsibility for gathering the current social-cultural, political, and economic data concerning the county. This committee provides the central holdings or library of information about the community and acts as a repository for the materials and data gathered from surveying the current and ongoing issues affecting the quality of life of the community.

The environmental scanning committee at JSCC discovered several major concepts about its service area; these included a high rate of adult illiteracy, a low-wage economy but rapidly expanding swine and poultry industries, and a rising and increasing awareness of the potential of conflict between developing industries and environmental concerns (for example, swine waste). While the citizenry was highly participative, their political preferences were usually reactive and conservative; and although industries demonstrated growth and expansion, work force training had not kept up. Literacy, low wages, need for training, and potential conflict over resources were all critical issues for Duplin County. The question of how to prioritize the issues and to plan for them was indeed serious. Developing a five-year plan to address these issues, immediate attention was given to adult basic education (literacy). A seventy-member coalition was formed that included leaders in the college and community; stakeholders were identified and asked to join the group, and, finally, essential members of targeted publics were included. A professional facilitator was hired to move the group from diversity to collaboration until a coalition was formed. Then, in a series of meetings, the issue of literacy was studied and broken down into component parts (and study groups); a plan for action in the community was developed.

Now Duplin County is addressing the issue of adult illiteracy and plans to monitor, adjust, and evaluate this plan for several years. The integration of this program into the community by a coalition of college and community people is an example of civic accountability through community-based programming. Other colleges in South Carolina, Maryland, and Virginia are involved in the program as well.

Southside Virginia Community College (SVCC) is also engaged in the process of community-based programming. Long known for their excellent prison service programs, the college has become very attached to improving and expanding their community role outside the boundaries of providing educational programs as community service. Like other rural areas in the south, work force preparedness is a critical issue and need in that community. SVCC has developed a Community-Based Programming Management Team as their first effort to address this issue more precisely. Now that an issue has been selected, a coalition of critical college and community actors will be named.

Technical College of Lowcountry (TCLC) in Beaufort, South Carolina has also established an ACCLAIM Management Team. Economic development through human resource development is the issue chosen for college-community partnership, analysis, and resolution. ACCLAIM faculty and staff continue to meet with the TCLC group as consultants to pursue study, analysis, and mapping of the area. James Sprunt Community College has acted as adviser and consultant as well. Because much of the area is economically depressed, the college was confronted with the need for transportation for members of target publics; the college collaborated with the Lowcountry Office of Government and Regional Transport Authority to provide transportation for these critical team players.

At another end of the training schedule for ACCLAIM colleges is Hagerstown Junior College (HJC) in Maryland. Recently trained in the tasks of community-based programming, the college has committed to reexamining their mission statement and to naming an environmental scanning committee to study their service area. In the first stages of the programs' tasks, HJC also visited other ACCLAIM colleges for additional training.

Conclusion

College-community relationships are not new for community colleges, but in this renewed drive to become more accountable the movement has the potential for elevating the community college to a greater position of centrality in the affairs of its community than ever attained by any other educational institution in America. Community colleges can become a significant force in helping the people in their service areas emphasize such basic precepts as self-initiative, self-reliance, resolve, and the fierce belief in and commitment to independence and democracy upon which the nation was founded—the values that make American citizenship the envy of the world. And in doing so they will practice civic accountability.

References

Bellah, R. N., Madsen, R., Sullivan, W. M., Swidler, A., and Tipton, S. M. *Habits of the Heart: Individualism and Commitment in American Life.* Berkeley: University of California Press, 1985.

Bellah, R. N., Madsen, R., Sullivan, W. M., Swidler, A., and Tipton, S. M. *The Good Society.* New York: Knopf, 1991.

Boone, E. J. *Developing Programs in Adult Education.* Englewood Cliffs, N.J.: Prentice-Hall, 1985.

Boone, E. J. *Community-Based Programming: An Opportunity and Imperative for the Community College.* Raleigh: The Academy for Community College Leadership Advancement, Innovation, and Modeling, North Carolina State University, 1992.

Boyle, P. G. *Planning Better Programs.* New York: McGraw-Hill, 1981.

Cohen, A. M. *Dateline 1979: Heretical Concepts for the Community College.* Beverly Hills, Calif.: Glencoe Press, 1969.

Cohen, A. M., and Brawer, F. B. *The American Community College.* (2nd ed.) San Francisco: Jossey-Bass, 1991.

College Council Meeting. Unpublished minutes. James Sprunt Community College, May 27, 1993.

Commission on the Future of Community Colleges. *Building Communities: A Vision for a New Century.* Washington, D.C.: American Association of Community Colleges, 1988. (ED 307 012)

Cyert, R. *The American Economy.* New York: Free Press, 1983.

Dalgaard, K. A., and others. *Issues Programming in Extension.* Minneapolis: Minnesota Extension Service, 1986.

Drucker, P. *Managing in Turbulent Times.* New York: HarperCollins, 1980.

Etzioni, A. *A Responsive Society: Collected Essays on Guiding Deliberate Social Change.* San Francisco: Jossey-Bass, 1991.

Etzioni, A. *The Spirit of Community: Rights, Responsibilities, and the Communitarian Agenda.* New York: Crown, 1993.

Gleazer, E. J. "After the Boom . . . What Now for the Community Colleges?" *Community and Junior College Journal,* Dec./Jan. 1974, *44,* 6–11.

Gleazer, E. J. *The Community College: Values, Vision and Vitality.* Washington, D.C.: American Association of Community and Junior Colleges, 1980.

Gollattscheck, J. F., Harlacher, E. L., Roberts, E., and Wygal, B. R. *College Leadership for Community Renewal: Beyond Community-Based Education.* San Francisco: Jossey-Bass, 1976.

Gutmann, A. *Democratic Education.* Princeton, N.J.: Princeton University Press, 1987.

Harlacher, E. "Critical Requirements for the Establishment of Effective Junior College Programs of Community Services." Unpublished Ed.D. dissertation, University of California, Los Angeles, 1965.

Harlacher, E. *The Community Dimension of the Community College.* Englewood Cliffs, N.J.: Prentice-Hall, 1969.

Harlacher, E. G., and Gollattscheck, J. F. (eds.). *Implementing Community-Based Education.* New Directions for Community Colleges, no. 21. San Francisco: Jossey-Bass, 1978.

Keller, G. *Academic Strategies*. Baltimore: Johns Hopkins University Press, 1983.

McClenney, K., LeCroy, N., and LeCroy, J. *Building Communities Through Strategic Planning*. Washington, D.C.: American Association of Junior and Community Colleges, 1991.

McGuire, K. B. *State of the Art in Community-Based Education in the American Community College*. Washington, D.C.: American Association of Junior and Community Colleges, 1988.

Morrison, J. L., Renfro, W. L., and Boucher, W. I. *Future Research and the Strategic Planning Process: Implications for Higher Education*. (ASHE-ERIC Higher Education Research Report No. 9). Washington, D.C.: Association for the Study of Higher Education, 1984.

Myran, G. A. *Community Services in the Community College*. Washington, D.C.: American Association of Junior Colleges, 1969. (ED 037 202)

Myran, G. A. "Antecedents: Evolution of the Community-Based College." In E. G. Harlacher and J. F. Gollattscheck (eds.), *Implementing Community-Based Education*. New Directions for Community Colleges, no. 21. San Francisco: Jossey-Bass, 1978.

Pifer, A. "Community College and Community Leadership." *Community and Junior College Journal*, Apr. 1974, *44*, 23–26.

Taylor, C. *The Ethics of Authenticity*. Cambridge: Harvard University Press, 1992.

ROSEMARY GILLETT-KARAM is associate professor of higher education, adult and community college education, North Carolina State University, Raleigh.

In 1995 Kapi'olani Community College was awarded grant funds to integrate service into the multicultural writing curriculum. This service learning program focuses on service as the civic responsibility of an educated citizenry and explores how values of service are reflected in contemporary Hawai'i's multicultural society.

Integrating Service into a Multicultural Writing Curriculum

Robert W. Franco

In 1986, the American Association of Community Colleges brought together nineteen distinguished leaders in higher education to produce *Building Communities: A Vision For a New Century*. Their mission statement focused on excessive fragmentation, cultural separation, and racial tension in local communities across America. It emphasized that many neighborhoods and families had lost their cohesiveness and that an atomistic individualism was on the rise (Commission on the Future of Community Colleges, 1988).

Today, within these communities, neighborhoods, and families, growing numbers of youths are in "serious jeopardy from multiple risks" (Ianni, 1994, p. 8). These risks include poverty, child abuse, school failure, substance abuse, gang violence, early and unprotected intercourse, and teenage suicide. The data are staggering. The Carnegie Council on Adolescent Development estimates that about seven million youth between the ages of ten and seventeen are confronting one or more of these risk factors in their daily lives (Dryfoos, 1990). In 1989, the Fordham Institute reported a decline of almost 50 percent in the social well-being of children and youth in the 1970s and 1980s (Jennings, 1994). One to One Partnerships focused on the increasing number of socially and economically disadvantaged young people and reported that one million children drop out of school each year, 1.5 million run away from home annually, and that American industry will spend $2.5 billion annually on remedial education (One to One Partnerships, 1994).

The authors of *Building Communities* addressed partnerships for learning and emphasized the obligation of America's community colleges to serve a diverse student population, to solve the dropout problem, and to help students succeed in higher education. They asserted a powerful role for community colleges in shaping the American future: "As partners in a network of institutions they can help the least advantaged move into the mainstream of American life, serve students of all ages, and provide education, civic empowerment and social integration for a growing number of citizens" (Commission on the Future of Community Colleges, 1988, p. 10).

While the authors of *Building Communities* were deliberating, a national coalition of college and university presidents was also recognizing the need to educate students for civic responsibility through engagement in community service. They created *Campus Compact: The Project for Public and Community Service* and asserted:

> Working with people from different backgrounds and experiences fosters an appreciation for pluralism in our society, openness to new ideas, and a thoughtfulness about social, political, economic and ethical issues. Community service is at once humbling and empowering. . . . When community involvement has been integrated into academic study, we also find that we have added a new vigor and purpose to our faculty's teaching and our students' learning: service enhances the primary mission of the university. [President's Statement, June 1991].

America's community colleges must reach out to their communities, create working partnerships with service agencies, and develop learning experiences beyond the classroom. However, if building and serving communities is to be fully integrated in the community college, then service concepts, values, and practices must be integrated into classroom teaching and curriculum development. Integrating service learning into the curriculum will contribute mightily to its sustainability. Ben Barber speaks eloquently of the relationship between civic democracy, service, and teaching: "The literacy required to live in civil society, the competence to participate in democratic communities, the ability to think critically and act deliberately in a pluralistic world, the empathy that permits us to hear and thus accommodate others, all involve skills that must be acquired. Excellence is the product of teaching and is liberty's measure" (Barber, 1992, p. 4).

The Needs of the Community and the Community College: A Local Perspective

Kapi'olani Community College (KCC) is one of seven community colleges that, together with an employment training center, make up the community college system of the University of Hawai'i. KCC's primary service area is in east Honolulu; however, students from throughout O'ahu and the Neighbor Islands are generating growing enrollment demand. In 1987, enrollment at Kapi'olani was just over 5,300, whereas fall 1995 enrollment topped 7,700. The college's diverse population of Native Hawaiians, Pacific Islanders, Asian, and European Americans reflects the wider demography of contemporary Hawai'i.

In fall 1993, remedial and developmental English students constituted nearly 12 percent of the total student population. Within this population there are students with a tremendous diversity of historical and cultural experience. We find local-born Native Hawaiians, European Americans, and Asian Americans, as well as recent immigrants, who may have graduated from or dropped out of local high schools with very limited English skills. We also find a growing number of immigrants recently arrived from the Philippines, Vietnam, Laos, Western and American Samoa, and other Pacific Island societies. The vast majority of these students are confronting the multiple risk factors identified above as they adapt to a new campus and community. Many of them "possess the unique inner strength and resources to take on these individual and collective human struggles alone, while others may have a family member or teacher, a church or social agency providing support" (Ianni, 1994, p.13). Inner strength and social support play a crucial role in the academic success of all students.

Kapi'olani is developing a service learning program designed to integrate service learning into three well-established and faculty-driven cross-curricular emphases—Writing Across the Curriculum (WAC), Thinking and Reasoning (TRE), and Kapi'olani's Asia-Pacific Emphasis (KAPE). Service learning will provide a bridge linking faculty learning communities committed to these emphases. This new faculty community will contribute to the long-term sustainability of service learning at Kapi'olani.

The service learning program's mission is to build on the unique cultural capabilities of students in our diverse population and create stronger social support systems for individuals confronting multiple risks. We need to "recast risks to be feared into challenges to be faced" and see to it that no one faces them alone (Ianni, 1994, p. 20). Through community service and thoughtful reflection, students will help develop communities in east and central Honolulu, and empower themselves. As students, staff, and faculty explore service learning in the curriculum, they will discover a multiplicity of community service concepts, values, and practices useful in building a civil, multicultural public.

Program Implementation

In January 1995, Kapi'olani was named an AACC Learn and Serve College and awarded grant funds to begin integrating service into the multicultural writing curriculum. A minigrant proposal entitled "Palolo Pride" was funded by the Campus Compact Center for Community Colleges (CCCCC), and another minigrant entitled "Multicultural Readings" was funded by Hawai'i State Campus Compact.

On January 15, spring semester began and fifteen KCC faculty had completed their first syllabus revisions with service learning statements. Students were to provide at least twenty hours of service, maintain a journal reflecting on their experiences, and compose reflective essays in class. They would receive credit toward their course grades for service and reflection. Most of the students' service was coordinated through the Palolo Interagency Council, a network of forty-five agencies and organizations serving low-income families in Palolo Valley; the Rainbow Ohana Coalition, which provides drug prevention education for immigrant and refugee youth; Helping Hands Hawai'i, which coordinates volunteer services on the island of O'ahu; and Project Dana, which provides respite care for the elderly, as well as numerous clinics, hospitals, and schools.

The first set of integrated service learning courses follow a curricular track leading from remedial and developmental to college-level English. In ENG 9V and 21V (Remedial Reading), ENG 102 (College Reading), ESL 130 (College Composition for ESL students), and ENG 100 (College Composition), students are involved in reading, writing, and mentoring activities with at-risk youth from Palolo Homes, a low-income community of two thousand people in east Honolulu. The instructors for ENG 9V and 21V and ENG 102 used Hawai'i Campus Compact funds to purchase and establish a multicultural children's library. This is currently being used in a new Saturday morning reading program at Kaimuki Library. The ESL 100 service learning students are immigrant students who have successfully followed an ESL track to a college-level composition course. These students produce a newsletter entitled "Palolo Pride" (initially funded by CCCCC), which is used as an effective networking tool by Palolo agencies and for reporting on other service learning activities and community events in east Honolulu. ENG 100 students, after receiving training from the Center for Oral History at the University of Hawai'i, Manoa, collect life histories of elderly residents of Palolo Valley, and compose these into essays that value and validate the lives of their informants.

The second set of integrated courses enables students to complete their social science area requirements with a strong service learning experience. In Anthropology 200, Cultural Anthropology, a required course for KCC nursing students, service learning is integrated into the existing fieldwork requirement. Students work in the Fetu Ao Samoan HIV/AIDS prevention education program and operate an HIV/AIDS Hotline at the Waikiki Health Center. In Sociology 218, Social Problems, students serve at nonprofit organizations dealing with homelessness, hunger, spouse abuse, or drug rehabilitation. In Sociology 231, Juvenile Delinquency, students work with the Adult Friends for Youth and provide gang prevention education for fifth graders who will soon transfer to junior high school. In Psychology 170, Psychology of Adjustment, students work through the Rainbow Ohana Coalition, or at day-care, low-intensity mental health clinics.

A third set of integrated courses will enable students to complete humanities area requirements with a strong service learning orientation. Students in Philosophy 102, Asian Traditions, and Philosophy 250, Ethics in Health Care, will provide volunteer service in community organizations and reflect on the philosophical basis of service and ethics in various Asian traditions. In History 152, World Civilizations, students will provide service in local homes for the elderly. These students also collect, reflect upon, and compose multicultural stories based on oral historical interviews with respected elders.

Service learning is also being integrated into our honors seminar, Honors 150, Global Village or Villages: Communication, Technology and Multiculturalism. Phi Theta Kappa students will complete their service requirement by working on the Polynesian Voyaging Society's Multimedia Education Project. This project explores Polynesian sailing techniques and traditions and will produce curriculum materials for KCC's Hawaiian language program and the public schools. Native Hawaiian students in second-year Hawaiian language courses are currently providing service to the Native Hawaiian preschool language-immersion programs.

Botany, nursing, and respiratory therapy professors have also integrated service learning opportunities into their course syllabi. Students in Botany 105, Ethnobotany, and Botany 130, Plants in the Hawaiian Environment, will provide service at the Lyon Arboretum. In Nursing 253, Mental Health/Psychiatric Nursing, students will provide services in family shelters, elderly long-term care facilities, disabled children's hospitals, and hospice care. Dozens of students in respiratory therapy courses serve at asthma camps, teach about tobacco use and cancer risks, and educate about the effects of HIV/AIDS on the respiratory system.

In spring 1996, with new funding from Hawai'i State Campus Compact, we will initiate a program entitled "Service and Science: Visions of Enrichment in Palolo Valley." Faculty teaching anatomy and physiology, astronomy, oceanography, botany, math, and business computing will have their service learning students involved in enrichment tutoring at Jarrat and Kaimuku Intermediate School. This tutoring will involve homework, library research, and field trips.

Our service learning model builds on three multicultural components. First, students learn to work across cultures in Honolulu neighborhoods. Second, the elderly they serve have the wisdom of the ages. Third, by working with younger adolescents and children, they are like older brothers and sisters teaching their younger siblings. These latter two components model the enculturation and socialization processes found in Native Hawaiian, Pacific, Asian, and in fact, all human cultures.

As of January 1996, we have at least one faculty member from every liberal arts and vocational education department practicing service learning. By May 1996, more than six hundred students will have learned and served in Honolulu's neighborhoods and communities. These students will have worked across cultures, generations, and genders, and they will have written substantial reflective journals based on their service experience. They will have learned from the elders and taught the younger generations useful educational and life lessons.

Service Learning to Explore America's Communities

In March 1995, Kapi'olani was named a mentor college in the National Endowment for the Humanities/AACC project "Exploring America's Communities: Quest for Common Ground." This project is part of the larger NEH national initiative, "A National Conversation on American Pluralism and Identity." As participants in this project, Kapi'olani faculty will share their experiences developing the college's international/multicultural Asian-Pacific emphasis. We will also share our most recent development—the integration of service learning into the Asian-Pacific multicultural curriculum—and how we use critical reflective writing to explore Honolulu's neighborhoods and communities.

Ethnicity is a major concept for exploring the history and character of American communities. Ethnicity, like the concepts of race and nationality, is always a boundary-marking concept; that is, it is an oppositional category. Culture is another concept useful for exploring the character of our communities. Within a population, in a bounded geographic area, culture is those essential shared values, beliefs, and norms that are communicated from generation to generation. Culture is not an oppositional category; it is specific to a place and changes over time.

The Native Hawaiian experience provides an excellent example of the important difference between ethnicity and culture as concepts for discussing the character of American communities. About A.D. 100, human beings arrived on these islands. Over the course of the next seventeen hundred years, they adapted an environmentally sensitive and politically complex society. At the heart of ancient Hawaiian culture were such concepts and values as 'ohana, extended family; aloha, welcome, kindness, love; ali'i, chiefs of many hierarchical statuses; ahupua'a, land division with shared resources from the mountains to the sea; lawelawe, to serve, work for, minister to, attend to, to treat, as the sick.

These central cultural concepts and values were developed in deep, rich agricultural valleys and managed by a chiefly structure that by the end of the nineteenth century approached the complexity of a state system. Individuals living in these valleys probably perceived their identity as family members within a system of related chiefly families.

In 1778, Captain James Cook arrived at Hawai'i Island, and asked, "What is the name of this island?" The people replied, "Owhyee." Cook wrote back to England and reported that the name of these islands was "Owhyee," and the inhabitants became "Hawaiians." At this exact point, people living the 'ohana-ali'i culture of these islands became an ethnic group, categorically different from Cook's British crew. The "Hawaiians" needed a concept to categorically distinguish themselves from these newcomers, so they called them "haoles." Ha means "without," and ole means "breath." The newcomers were speaking a different language and thus were without "voice." The first people of these islands developed a culture unique to this place, and that culture developed over time. From 1778 to the present, the terms Hawaiians or Native Hawaiians have been used to refer to all the native people of these islands. Hawaiians is an ethnic term, categorically opposed to the ethnic term haole. Haole was later changed to Caucasian, a race-based term adapted from Caucasoid.

Thus, from a social science perspective, it is important to distinguish people practicing 'ohana-ali'i culture in the many valleys and islands of this archipelago from "Native Hawaiians," an ethnic concept rooted in the European contact experience and growing stronger in the context of European-American oppression.

Today, Native Hawaiians have developed a culture, largely shaped by traditional values, ethnic opposition, and economic and political exploitation. They are now actively building their communities, and they are looking to pre-ethnic cultural values to provide direction in this rebuilding. KCC, through its curriculum and its service learning program, can encourage Native Hawaiian students to develop values of service (lawelawe) to help build their communities.

In contemporary Hawai'i, we have ethnic opposition, most strikingly in two areas: in the relations between Native Hawaiians and other groups, and in ethnically rooted youth gang activity. Nevertheless, compared to many states and nations, Hawai'i is a relatively successful multicultural society. Many of the peoples and cultures of contemporary Hawai'i have service values that provide clear direction in community development. Many communities have used their traditional family values to build diverse and distinctive communities with the spirit of aloha. In sum, our ethnic groups are not all "in opposition" to one another. We can understand and appreciate cultural values emerging from different traditions.

Conclusion

At Kapi'olani, our service learning program focuses on service as the civic responsibility of an educated citizenry; it explores Asian and Pacific traditional (pre-ethnic) values of service and how those values are reflected in contemporary Hawai'i's multicultural society. This exploration is of great relevance for American communities in other states where ethnic opposition as well as atomistic individualism is resulting in levels of community fragmentation and crisis that blur, even blind, any vision of civic democracy. Over the years, in African-American, Hispanic, Asian-American, and Pacific-American communities, traditional or pre-ethnic service values have, to some degree, been displaced by the experience of subservience and servitude. Today, for some individuals, service-sector employment works against the formation of an empowering concept of service for civic democracy. All communities have their own strengths—in particular, pre-ethnic service values—with which to build themselves, and through this community development they can make greater contributions to building an American civic democracy with civil diversity.

References

Barber, B. R. An Aristocracy of Everyone: The Politics of Education and the American Future. New York: Oxford University Press, 1992, p. 4.

Commission on the Future of Community Colleges. Building Communities: A Vision for a New Century. Washington, D.C.: American Association of Community Colleges, 1988. (ED 307 012)

Dryfoos, J. G. *Adolescents at Risk*. New York: Oxford University Press, 1990.

Ianni, F. *Social, Cultural, and Behavioral Contexts of Mentoring*. New York: Institute for Urban and Minority Education, Columbia University, 1994.

Jennings, L. "Fordham Institute's Index Documents Steep Decline in Children's and Youth's Social Health Since 1970." *Education Week*, Nov. 1, 1989, p. 9. Cited in F. Ianni, 1994, p. 9.

One to One Partnerships. *Mobilizing for the Next Generation*. Washington D.C.: One to One Partnerships, 1994, p. 4.

"President's Statement." *Campus Compact: The Project for Public and Community Service*. Third draft, June 1991.

ROBERT W. FRANCO is associate professor of anthropology at Kapi'olani Community College, University of Hawai'i.

This chapter presents additional educational programs related to civic literacy and community services. The importance of providing a community-centered focus for each curriculum is also discussed.

Sources and Information: Current Programming in Civic Literacy and Community Services

Janel Ann Soulé Henriksen

Current research into the scope of civic education in the community college, as well as programs designed to assist members of the community to understand and negotiate the complex issues of our urban society, is, to date, limited. This review of literature highlights related work that is currently in place in community colleges throughout our nation. Programs meeting the needs of a diverse population of postsecondary education consumers lend evidence to the fact that although attention to civic education is limited, it is growing and is taking its rightful place within the community college system.

Civic Responsibility, Civic Learning, and General Education

Higginbottom (1991) presents an historical account of the implementation of civic education into the general education curriculum of community colleges since the 1940s. He notes that in the middle part of the twentieth century, few studies had been conducted on civic education but that there was much evidence to support civic education's incorporation into general education. For example, Higginbottom states that as early as 1915, A. A. Gray of the University of California believed the central goal of education to be the "preparation for citizenship and not for the higher educational institutions" (p. 414). Such sentiment, notes Higginbottom, extended itself through the 1960s, as Lamar Johnson encouraged general education to focus on "the knowledge, skills, and attitudes needed by an individual to be an effective person, a family member, a worker, and a citizen" (p. 415).

When confronted with the push toward vocational and occupational education and a transfer function, the community colleges found themselves in flux, caused by the belief that America needed to maintain a competitive technological edge and by the interests of corporations, business, and four-year institutions in steering community college students away from a traditional two-year degree program. Current thinking stresses the development of more civic- and problem-oriented and experimental community college curricula.

Given that community colleges are "democracy's colleges," open to all who desire educational experiences beyond secondary education, Higginbottom discusses the general education curriculum at five different colleges that acknowledge the importance of creating an educated and thoughtful citizenry. Included in his discussion are descriptions of Cedar Valley College, Texas, which operates a "skills for living" program, to verse students in "relationships, economic, social and political roles, and orientations" (Higginbottom, 1991, p. 433). This college considers "preparation for citizenship" an important component for curricular reform. Miami-Dade Community College, Florida, acknowledges civic purpose as a vital goal in the general education provided to their quickly growing student body. Higginbottom notes, however, that at this particular college, practice may not always follow carefully constructed theory. At Miami-Dade, citizenship within the academic plan refers to problem solving and decision making, and the role of the person within a diverse community is not emphasized. Los Medanos College, California, has established a general education platform that combines the aspects of learning, society, and schooling. The curriculum, thus constructed, was geared to be an education to benefit the "survival of the individual and society . . . integrated and interdisciplinary, lead learners to explore ethical aspects of societal issues, and advance the belief that knowledge should lead to action" (Higginbottom, 1991, p. 447).

Following Higginbottom's comprehensive study, a few other colleges began discussing their curricular and academic role within a diverse citizenry. One college within the Los Angeles Community College District presents a description of citizenship programs in the heart of its city that currently are managing immigration and racial tensions. Fujimoto (1994) guides the reader through the history of developing an Amnesty Education program at Los Angeles Mission College.

In 1987, Los Angeles community colleges took steps that eventually led to the establishment of the Southern California Community College Amnesty Network. Its primary goal was the implementation of amnesty education programs on campuses. These programs were created to help a group identified as "New Californians," who shared common characteristics such as long work hours, low income, and limited English proficiency. Outreach services to assist this unique population of community college students were needed; the goal was to ease the transition of this population of New Californians to life in the United States. The work of this advocacy group led to the adoption by the Los

Angeles Community College District trustees of a policy mandating that amnesty education be offered on all campuses within the district. Fujimoto also discusses funding, enrollment, curriculum, and staffing, and provides a detailed discussion of the administrative concerns and processes that have guided the implementation of such a program at one of the colleges within the Los Angeles Community College District.

Community-Based Programming and Service Learning

The true benefits of student involvement within their community is best documented by Berson, who cited a study by Allan Luks, *The Healing Power of Doing Good*. Luks found that volunteers who work with an organization are more likely to continue regular volunteer activities. Those who participate in community service programs report "good feelings" that maintain good health and happiness (Berson, 1994).

Community-based programming within the community college forum is defined and described by Boone (1992b). It is a process that requires colleges to lead community members and organizations through a series of tasks in order to define the problems in need of resolution and collaboratively engage in solving these community-based conflicts.

As the catalyst for community programming, Boone feels, community colleges must gather the focus and attention of community leaders and others to a specific problem or issue in need of a positive resolution, stimulate participants to work collaboratively to analyze the issue and agree upon an effective solution, and provide continual support to the selected team in their efforts to put their solutions into practice. Issues appropriately confronted by community-based programming have three components: 1) they exist throughout the society; 2) they are inherently problematic in that their root—economic, political, social, or technological—is cause for much argument between people of different opinions; and 3) their resolution requires mediation or negotiation (Boone, 1992b, p. 3). Collaboration is key for the effective resolution of such societal issues.

Vaughan (1991) provides an excellent historical review of community services as part of the community college structure. In 1925, Leonard V. Koos and Walter Crosby Eells recognized the need for "junior colleges" to be sensitive to the concerns and issues faced by their communities. Perhaps precocious for his day, Eells is said to have believed that "serving community needs meant going beyond serving the needs of the regular student body" (Vaughan, 1991, p. 24). As part of the democratizing process of the community college structure, the President's Commission on Higher Education in 1946 suggested that community colleges bring education to all people. Based on this historical perspective, Vaughan contends that community services have long been an instrumental component of community colleges. Despite its rich history, however, community service is, according to Vaughan, faced with an identity crisis, caused largely by the fact that community colleges continually are being challenged to offer more services to a wider population of people. Night courses, prison education, child care centers, geriatric education, and business and industry liaisons are but a few of the diverse programs community colleges attempt to provide, often at the expense of losing sight of their goals.

Vaughan presents other reasons for the diminishing profile of community service within the community college: 1) community service advocates offer courses often viewed as "frivolous" by college administrators and other faculty; 2) funding has been curtailed for many community service programs; 3) few people are willing to create innovative programming "gambles"; and 4) the recession has caused community colleges to focus more rigorous attention on job training and vocational skills. In addition, community service programs that are popular and in demand are often viewed with a jealous eye by those faculty members "struggling to fill empty seats" (Vaughan, 1991, p. 25).

Vaughan's bleak review of current obstacles to community service concludes, however, with suggestions for revitalizing such programming. He suggests that community services should be brought into mainstream, general education instruction. In addition, community service leaders should direct more of their attention on program planning and "serve as the innovative arm of the instructional program" (Vaughan, 1991, p. 26). Finally, full-time counselors should be assigned to community service divisions, and community service programs should be careful to maintain and insist upon institutional integrity.

Two years after his rather frustrated look at the status of community service programs in 1991, Vaughan revisited the issue in 1993, providing energetic ideas about how community-based programming can be effectively implemented. He poses the question, "Where does the community turn in its attempt to improve the quality of life for its citizens?" The answer is the community college. Vaughan firmly believes that "community college leaders can take an important step toward helping communities identify and resolve issues of major importance if their colleges function as both leaders and catalysts in their communities" (1993, p. 1). To do this, colleges are placed in a mediating and problem-solving position among organizations, institutions, and leaders who are committed to resolving community conflict.

Vaughan's ideas, although written as a call to arms, may not be realistic when the necessary internal forces and commitment within educational institutions are not considered. Boone (1992b) points out that few mechanisms exist that will foster continuing relationships between colleges and community organizations and institutions. He writes that what is needed is a community organization that will "act as a leader and catalyst in bringing groups together to identify issues and seek solutions" (1992b, p. 1). He feels the community college is an appropriate institution to fulfill that role.

Perhaps because he is a bit more specific, Boone (1992a, 1992b) offers a more concrete plan of action for colleges interested in developing community-based programs on campus than do other authors in this field. He outlines many "procedural tasks" that community colleges should follow, including (1) developing a definition and mission for community-based programming; (2) increasing knowledge about the community's social and political climate;

(3) ranking and prioritizing current community issues that need to be addressed, and the constituencies affected by these issues; (4) initiating communication with civic leaders to target these issues and provide leadership in developing and following through with a plan of action; and (5) assessing continued progress and presenting final results to all participants.

Berson (1994) presents additional suggestions for creating service learning programs within the community college setting. Based on experiences at her home campus, Broward Community College, Florida, Berson suggests that initial steps should include forming an advisory committee of interested students, faculty, staff, and community-based corporations for the purpose of structuring service learning programs. Once programs are in place, Berson recommends that colleges consider documenting students' community-based learning experiences. To do so would create an information base for potential employers seeking students with skills developed through such programs and would establish a method by which to recognize students' outstanding participation within the community. Of course, funding these programs is almost always a major concern. In this area, Berson advises that colleges not "leave any stone unturned," and urges community colleges to seek the assistance of federal and state agencies as well as institutions geared toward supporting community service programs, such as the Corporation on National and Community Service (1994, p. 18).

Other authors have submitted ERIC documents that report the progress and success of their respective community-based programs. McNutt (1994) describes the Technical College of Lowcountry's participation as one of eight pilot colleges in a program known as the Academy for Community College Leadership Advancement, Innovation, and Modeling (ACCLAIM). This program is designed to promote community-based programs through (1) continuing education programs for faculty, administrators, and community college governance officials; (2) a doctoral degree program in "community college leadership" for participants, with fellowships awarded to twelve to fourteen students; (3) the development, testing, and dissemination of community-based programming written materials, guides, texts, and management tools; and (4) a faculty enrichment and renewal program designed to help professors in university education programs that provide graduate degree programs for community college leaders.

LeCroy and Tedrow (1993) describe a foundation-sponsored program designed to address troubling issues affecting surrounding communities. In 1991, the Hitachi Foundation in conjunction with the League for Innovation in the Community College established a program that assists community colleges in planning and conducting community forums to discuss these issues. The program also assists community colleges in "building the capacity of the nine community colleges and communities that participate in the . . . project to deal with real problems" (LeCroy and Tedrow, 1993, p. 1). The goal of this joint effort by the League and Hitachi was to create a program that could be replicated by other campuses. When these nine colleges followed the guidelines as established by the program, many success stories were reported, as were some difficulties, including problems inherent in focusing on one topic, building necessary community and college support, underestimating the amount of time and work needed to conduct such forums, and difficulties in reaching a sense of "closure" and follow-up. Despite these obstacles, the authors write that such forums as designed by this joint effort "helped . . . local communities confront wide-ranging and sometimes controversial topics, increase their understanding of these issues, and create at least the beginnings of a framework for problem solving" (LeCroy and Tedrow, 1993, p. 2).

Collin County Community College (1991) utilized community service programming not only to introduce students to the benefits of community service but also to help students develop practical occupational skills. The program, Students Utilizing Collin County's Educational and Service Systems (SUCCESS), provides student participants vocational and technical education; the students also gain service learning experience working for community agencies. Students with diverse technical abilities, maturity levels, and educational abilities are eligible to participate in this program, often receiving academic credit for their work. Collin County's extensive documentation of this program provides suggestions for marketing the program, an outline of the program's organizational structure, and a curriculum designed to help students maximize their community service education.

Conclusion

Understanding the need for colleges and their surrounding communities to work together to address social issues and to help citizens appreciate their important role in a diverse and often troubled society, it is little wonder that so many community colleges have enthusiastically structured community-based programming into their curriculum. Activities designed to help individuals gain a sense of community and civic pride have proven successful. Civic literacy is often a component of general education. However, there are still those who caution community colleges not to lose sight of the importance of involving citizens in their work. Gollattscheck (1991) recommended that community colleges look beyond traditional continuing and community education programs and seek out partnerships with surrounding industry and organizations to further enhance community colleges' ability to be "democracy's college." Indeed, Gollattscheck's 1991 work may have heralded the advent of a new breed of community services and civic literacy, intended to highlight the benefits colleges can bring to their communities.

References

Berson, J. S. "A Marriage Made in Heaven: Community Colleges and Service Learning." *Community College Journal*, June/July 1994, *64* (6), 14–19.

Boone, E. J. *Guidelines for Community Colleges to Follow in Community-Based Programming.* Raleigh: Academy for Community College Leadership Advancement, Innovation, and Modeling, North Carolina State University, 1992a.

Boone, E. J. *Community-Based Programming: An Opportunity and Imperative for the Community College.* Raleigh: Academy for Community College Leadership Advancement, Innovation, and Modeling, North Carolina State University, 1992b. (ED 354 975)

Collin County Community College. *SUCCESS: A Model Cooperative Education-Based Community Service Program.* Austin, Tex.: Texas Higher Education Coordinating Board, 1991. (ED 344 013)

Fujimoto, J. *Fulfilling the Promise: From Amnesty to Citizenship. Part I, the Los Angeles Mission College Experience.* Los Angeles, Calif.: Monograph of the California Community College Educators for New Californians, Los Angeles, Calif., Aug. 1994.

Gollattscheck, J. F. "Will Success Destroy Community Services and Continuing Education? or What Do You Do with the Revolutionaries After You've Won the Revolution?" *Community Services Catalyst,* Summer 1991, *21* (3), 28–31.

Higginbottom, G. H. *The Civic Ground of Collegiate General Education and the Community College.* New York: The Institute for Community College Research, Broome Community College, 1991. (ED 338 277)

LeCroy, N., and Tedrow, B. "Catalyst for Community Change: Helping to Address Critical Issues." *Leadership Abstracts,* May 1993, *6* (5). (ED 367 428)

McNutt, A. S. "Moving Teaching and Learning into the Twenty-First Century Through Community-Based Programming." Paper presented at the 74th Annual Convention of the American Association of Community Colleges, Washington, D.C., April 6–9, 1994. (ED 369 439)

Vaughan, G. B. "Community Services New Frontier: Establishing the Ties That Bind." *Community Services Catalyst,* Summer 1991, *21* (3), 24–27.

Vaughan, G. B. *Community-Based Programming: The Community College as Leader and Catalyst.* Southern Association of Community, Junior, and Technical Colleges Occasional Paper, Mar. 1993, *11* (1). (ED 354 974)

JANEL ANN SOULÉ HENRIKSEN is a research associate at the ERIC Clearinghouse for Community Colleges, Los Angeles, California. She is also a doctoral candidate at the University of California, Los Angeles.

INDEX

Ordering Information

New Directions for Community Colleges is a series of paperback books that provides expert assistance to help community colleges meet the challenges of their distinctive and expanding educational mission. Books in the series are published quarterly in Spring, Summer, Fall, and Winter and are available for purchase by subscription and individually.

Subscriptions for 1996 cost $51.00 for individuals (a savings of more than 25 percent over single-copy prices) and $81.00 for institutions, agencies, and libraries. Please do not send institutional checks for personal subscriptions. Standing orders are accepted. (For subscriptions outside of North America, add $7.00 for shipping via surface mail or $25.00 for air mail. Orders *must be prepaid* in U.S. dollars by check drawn on a U.S. bank or charged to VISA, MasterCard, or American Express.)

Single copies cost $19.00 plus shipping (see below) when payment accompanies order. California, New Jersey, New York, and Washington, D.C. residents please include appropriate sales tax. Canadian residents add GST and any local taxes. Billed orders will be charged shipping and handling. No billed shipments to post office boxes. (Orders from outside North America *must be prepaid* in U.S. dollars by check drawn on a U.S. bank or charged to VISA, MasterCard, or American Express.)

Shipping (Single Copies Only): $10.00 and under, add $2.50; to $20.00, add $3.50; to $50.00, add $4.50; to $75.00, add $5.50; to $100.00, add $6.50; to $150.00, add $7.50; over $150.00, add $8.50.

Discounts for quantity orders are available. Please write to the address below for information.

All orders must include either the name of an individual or an official purchase order number. Please submit your order as follows:
    Subscriptions: specify series and year subscription is to begin
    Single copies: include individual title code (such as CC82)

Mail all orders to:
    Jossey-Bass Publishers
    350 Sansome Street
    San Francisco, California 94104-1342

For subscription sales outside of the United States, contact any international subscription agency or Jossey-Bass directly.